OUR WORK, OUR LIVES, OUR WORDS

Our Work, Our Lives, Our Words

Edited by

**Leonore Davidoff
and
Belinda Westover**

**BARNES & NOBLE BOOKS
TOTOWA, NEW JERSEY**

First published in the U.S.A. 1986 by
BARNES & NOBLE BOOKS
81, Adams Drive, Totowa,
New Jersey, 07512

Printed in Great Britain

Library of Congress Cataloging-in-Publication Data
Our work, our lives, our words.
1. Women—Employment—Great Britain—History—20th century.   2. Work and family—Great Britain—History—20th century.   I. Davidoff, Leonore   II. Westover, Belinda.
HD6135.095   1986   331.4'0941   86–14046
ISBN 0–389–20655–5
ISBN 0–389–20656–3 (pbk.)

For Brenda Corti, whose warmth and enthusiasm has helped so many students and staff on the University of Essex social history programme over the years

Contents

Preface

After the relative calm of mid-Victorian prosperity, England of the 1880s was once again in turmoil. This rapid pace of change was to continue into the new century. The generations growing up between 1880 and 1914 were experiencing a merging of new and old, from industrial processes to the questioning of woman's place. The women whose lives form the substance of this book were born during these decades. Their lives should be taken as representative of millions of others who have left no personal records. For all of them, their formative years were touched in some way by the Great War. All lived through the experience of a divided nation in the inter-war years and their middle age was shadowed by yet another major war. While each was a unique individual, collectively they form the story of the lives of English women which links us with our own past. In this sense, each may be taken as a typical 'girl of the period'.

All the contributors to this volume have interviewed women born during those decades and oral evidence is an important linking theme of the chapters. Oral material is a valuable source for historians generally, but it is particularly important for the history of women's work and the family. In this field of study, documentary sources are often partial and inadequate. Not only is the experience of women filtered through the eyes of social commentators, most of who were men, but there are substantial gaps in the documentary evidence about what women were doing. Women's lives have been considered trivial and unchanging and thus unworthy of serious historical study, particularly in their domestic role. Therefore we know little about family life and about the distinct stages of women's life cycle. Even in the more public arena of the workplace, documentary sources tell us little or nothing about the actual work experience of women, the choices available to them or influences on their initial choice of occupation, for instance the mother's role in a girl's important first step into the wider world. Most importantly, oral history enables us to make the link between work and family life. Women do not experience their lives in compartments of home, work and leisure but mesh employment with domestic commitments. In this way their work fits around their lives, unlike the pattern regarded as normal because it applies to men. Finally, oral history does not simply tell the story of individual lives, it helps to tell the story of a generation and makes the link between people's life experiences and the wider historical context.

The contributors to this book are themselves the daughters and granddaughters of the generation of women whose experience forms its subject matter. Most of us are part of the '1945 generation' who benefited from the improvements in health, 'welfare and educational opportunities brought about by the post-war welfare state. All were University of Essex graduate students or staff who began their study as mature students. The majority were in their 30s and 40s when the research upon which the contributions are based was carried out. Among themselves, the authors have fifteen children, and each has coped with the pressures of bringing up a family and caring for dependants while studying and working. In this respect our experience resembles that of the women we have interviewed and written about, and it is no accident that we chose to study women's history and women's work. Some of us have taught women's history in adult education and have often felt the need for a book like this which gives insights into women's everyday lives in the earlier part of our own century. Contrary to the opinion of many male historians, women's lives are varied and dynamic. Nevertheless, the lives of women in the generations before us, although very different from our own in many ways, have a similarity in that we too live within the constraints of a male-dominated society.

Leonore Davidoff and Belinda Westover describe the world into which these women were born; their education, the type of work available to them, living conditions, social life, patterns of birth, marriage and death. It discusses in some detail the typical nineteenth-century female occupation of domestic service. The following three chapters by Eve Hostettler, Belinda Westover and Joanna Bornat are concerned with working-class women. Work opportunities for them varied between monotony of long days in the textile mill, to the pick up and put down pattern of tailoring or the even more irregular harvest work in the spaces between cooking, cleaning and looking after children.

Frances Widdowson, Teresa Davy and Kay Sanderson talked to women fortunate enough to have family backing and education, who took up the new white-collar positions becoming available. The education they received and the opening of such work to women were due, in part, to the efforts of late nineteenth-century feminists who understood the crucial importance of paid work as a basis for women's independence. All the contributions show, however, how difficult and at what cost to their families and themselves, was the effort to fit women's lives into the world of paid work. The anonymous structures of the factory or office were alien to many women's experience and they were almost always at a disadvantage compared with the male worker in terms of pay, working conditions and status. The final chapter, by Elizabeth Crosthwait, highlights these themes with the entry of women into the most masculine stronghold, the British army, during the First World War.

All the work in this volume originated in the Social History Programme of graduate research which has run since 1973 in the Sociology Department at the University of Essex: oral history and women's history have been special topics of study. We would like to thank those connected with the Programme: Brenda Corti, Judy Lown, Trevor Lummis and Paul Thompson, and the secretarial staff of the department, Carole Allington and Mary Girling. All real names of the women interviewed have been changed.

LEONORE DAVIDOFF
BELINDA WESTOVER

Notes on the Contributors

Joanna Bornat is an editor of the journal *Oral History* and worked for several years as educational director of a large national charity working for older people. She is Deputy Head of the ILEA Education Resource Unit for older people.

Elizabeth Crosthwait has worked for several years as a community worker in London.

Leonore Davidoff is a lecturer in social history in the Department of Sociology at the University of Essex. She teaches a graduate course in women's history and is the author of books and articles on domestic service, women and the family in nineteenth- and early twentieth-century Britain.

Teresa Davy qualified as a Careers Adviser in 1982 and worked for two years in schools in Hertfordshire. She works for the ILEA Careers Service in a south London Further Education college working with students who range from school-leavers to adults returning to education.

Eve Hostettler was born and brought up in Lincolnshire. She is employed on the Isle of Dogs in the heart of London's docklands, working with local residents on the recovery and preservation of their history.

Kay Sanderson is currently working on a research project at the University of East Anglia on the occupational and career differentiation of men and women and finishing her PhD.

Belinda Westover is working as part-time lecturer in social history at the University of Essex and for the Open University and is an editor of the journal *Life Stories*. She has also taught in adult education, including women's studies courses.

Frances Widdowson works in the Equal Opportunities Department of the National Union of Teachers. This work covers equal opportunities for pupils in schools, career development for women teachers and the active involvement of women in the union.

Acknowledgements

The author and publishers wish to thank the following who have kindly given permission for the use of copyright material:

The Controller of Her Majesty's Stationery Office for chart 'Economic Activity Rates for Married Females by Age 1921–1971' from *Women and Work: A Statistical Survey*.

International Labour Office for *The War and Women's Employment: The Experience of the United Kingdom and the United States*, Studies and Reports, New Series No. 1, Table 1, page 2, 'Numbers of Women Employed, July 1914–July 1918', ©1946, ILO, Geneva.

Every effort has been made to trace all the copyright-holders, but if any have been inadvertently overlooked the publishers will be pleased to make the necessary arrangement at the first opportunity.

1 'From Queen Victoria to the Jazz Age': Women's World in England, 1880–1939

**LEONORE DAVIDOFF and
BELINDA WESTOVER**

Working women do not experience a rigid division between their work and their family; between the 'public' and 'private' parts of their lives. Most of the contributors to this volume, for example, discuss how the family influenced the choice of employment of a young woman starting work in the early years of this century and how her experience of that work and levels of pay were structured around her expectation of domestic responsibilities.

It is true that the twentieth century offered new opportunities for unmarried women, both manual and non-manual. There was an expansion of work typecast as female. In contrast to domestic service, these jobs provided girls with the chance to work outside private homes and along side others. Thus the potential for solidarity based on common perceptions of their situation increased. Nevertheless, married women's place mainly continued within the casual home economy, their social circle confined to relatives, friends and neighbours (see the chapters by Westover and Hostettler).

A girl born in 1900 would expect to leave school at from 12 to 14 and start work immediately unless she was needed to help at home. Her choice of job would depend on her family's situation but also the opportunities in the area where she lived. For most girls this meant factory work if it was available, otherwise domestic service except for those few from middle class or the most prosperous working-class backgrounds who might aspire to shop, clerical work or teaching. The contributions to this volume show how some of these alternative occupations for women in the early twentieth century helped to structure their lives and how the women used these opportunities in relation to their feminine role.

All these young women started their adult lives steeped in a set of ideas which maintained that their final and proper place was in the home. By the end of the nineteenth century, a girl's goal was marriage and upon marriage she was ideally to be supported by a male breadwinner. The type of work she could expect to do, her expectations and actual work experience, were profoundly affected by this prevailing ideology. It had shaped girls' education and was enshrined in law, political institutions and social policy backed by religious doctrine. For example, many people, including parents, viewed factory work as unsuitable for girls and they were encouraged to enter domestic service which was held to be good training for future feminine role. The disapproving image of factory girls was derived from fear of sexual and economic independence whereas domestic service was supposed to give little opportunity to deviate from the accepted path.

The image of what women were supposed to do and be was transmitted to girls through a variety of forms. One of the most powerful was the education system which had started to expand in the 1860s. By 1890, education was both compulsory and free for children up to 13. A major aim of schools was to imbue working class children with what had become the middle class view of family functions and responsibilities.[1] The type of education girls received in the late nineteenth century sought to prepare them for their future as wives and mothers whereas boys were educated for their role in the labour market. Thus in addition to habits of cleanliness and obedience, girls were taught domestic subjects and needlework. It was considered natural that they should gravitate to jobs in personal services, millinery, tailoring and dressmaking.

The household with a male who supported, controlled and represented his dependant wife and children was the form of family on which the political and legal system was built. Married women had minimal rights over their children, their choice of residence, their own time or labour. Until the late nineteenth century, a married woman could be confined to the house by her husband and legally beaten (within reasonable limits). Until the Married Women's Property Act of 1884, a married woman had no right to own property and any money she earned belonged to her husband.[2]

Although by the beginning of the twentieth century, legal

changes had modified the position of married women, the view that wives were the property of their husbands lingered on and had important effects of womens' employment. Their position in the workforce as supplementary earners was framed by the assumption that they would marry and be supported by their husbands. However, the idea that an individual man would be the breadwinner was relatively new to the early nineteenth century. Before industrialisation advanced, all members of the family had been expected to contribute to the family subsistence or income. Later on, as home and the workplace became separated, married women were no longer expected to make a direct economic contribution to the household. Men were increasingly assumed to be earning a 'family wage'.[3] Low wages for women were justified by this expectation and kept them dependent on men while encouraging them to marry. Women were also expected to perform domestic tasks for men and children, a form of labour which had increased with a rising standard of living. In this way, men benefited both from higher wages and from the division of labour in the home. The earner of the family wage, the male breadwinner, was entitled to certain privileges in the household, for example, better food and more time after work for himself and he was usually spared the burden of domestic chores and childcare.

The experience of women in the late nineteenth century and early twentieth centuries was always coloured by these ideas. However, their everyday lives were not necessarily consistent with the prevailing norm of womanhood and this is particularly true for working-class women. In practice, many men simply did not earn enough to support a non-working wife and children, or others were unwilling to do so, and for many households, the family wage remained an ideal rather than reality. But the powerful hold of these ideas and the occupational divisions men and women they helped create, made it increasingly difficult for the wives, and sometimes even the daughters, of skilled workmen with aspirations to respectability, to be seen as wage earners.

When it was necessary for a woman to find work, she would often turn to casual, ill-paid jobs like cleaning, taking in lodgers, childminding and homework (see chapter by Westover). These activities were seen as both practical and acceptable extensions of their normal tasks. The double burden of housework, including childcare, and paid work meant that it was not easy in any case, for married women to take full-time jobs. Disincentives which made it difficult and unrewarding for married women to work for wages reinforced the expectation that they should not work. Finally, by the late nineteenth century, changes in attitudes to children had given greater importance to the mother's role. The burden of responsibility on the biological mother, the positive rewards of raising children and the feelings of guilt for not being constantly with her own children which was to be a feature of the twentieth century, had their origins in this period.

Social policy relating to women also reflected the prevailing assumptions about their role as wife and mother rather than wage earner and the belief that all families had a male breadwinner. This was first enshrined in public policy in the revised Poor Law of 1834 and was still true in the 1900s. Charles Booth had clearly demonstrated in his great study of London in the 1880s that the survival of the family often depended on the wife and children's earnings, yet it was still assumed that married women worked for 'pin money' to pay for luxuries.[4] The 1911 National Insurance Act, the first of its kind, excluded married women home workers from its unemployment provisions on the grounds that married women's earnings were not essential to the family economy. Women wage earners and their problems were not directly considered by officials from the start of welfare in keeping with the central aim of making men responsible for their families and increasing their motivation to remain steadily at work.[5]

Women remained among the poorest members of the population in the early twentieth century. They were more likely to be widowed because they married at a younger age than men and lived longer than their husbands. They were less likely to remarry once widowed, especially if they had young children or dependent relatives. Their earnings were much lower than those of men and their work opportunities more limited. Low pay made individual saving difficult and women were generally excluded from mutual savings institutions like Friendly Societies through which working men could protect themselves against sickness and old age. Not surprisingly, many elderly women were reduced to seeking help from family and friends or charity from voluntary societies. Throughout this period, the dreaded workhouse with its rigid institutional regime and implications of shameful failure cast a shadow over their lives.

Women gained far less than men from the post-1906 Liberal reforms when unemployment protection and sickness insurance were taken on by the state for the first time. Again, it was presumed that women would be taken care of within the family. The official attitude to women as secondary members of the workforce continued into the inter-war period in spite of the influx of women into new employment in light engineering and the clerical sector. For example, the Unemployment Insurance Act of 1922 contained a clause whereby 'extended benefit' was payable only to those genuinely seeking full-time employment but unable to obtain it. The chief effect of this test was to exclude married women from benefit. They were assumed to have less need for a full income than men and they were less likely to protest at its withdrawal. The official fear of the propensity of women to 'scrounge' blurred the extent of the problem whose very existence was never actually established.[6]

Change came with the Second World War. In drawing up his report in the early 1940s, William Beveridge was especially concerned that justice should be done to non-working housewives. Looking forward to the home-centred ideology of the 1950s and away from married women's employment during the Second World War, he proposed that, in return for the contributions made by their husbands, married women should receive maternity benefits and widowed, separated or divorced allowances. Beveridge argued that the work of housewives was as important socially and economically as waged work and should be given equal recognition in the social security system.

In the late nineteenth century, the state had gradually become more closely involved with the care of children, shifting from the traditional view that they were the sole responsibility of their families alone. Infant welfare in particular became a national issue after the Boer War at the turn of the century, because of the attention drawn to the poor quality of army recruits. A campaign began to 'glorify, dignify and purify motherhood'. It was widely accepted that a fit and healthy nation was necessary for the maintenance of the Empire and that mothers, who were responsible for the next generation, needed to be educated towards that responsibility. Infant mortality in particular was seen as a failure of motherhood. Although it was clear both to those who carried out the social surveys of the early twentieth century and to women's groups at the time, that poverty was a major factor in infant mortality and ill health, government officials went to considerable lengths to avoid confronting the issue of poverty directly. Instead mothers were to be taught to make the best of whatever resources they had and were encouraged to realise the value of self-help. By 1939, ante-natal care, skilled attendance in childbirth, infant welfare clinics, health visitors and hospital facilities for women giving birth, were among the services available, although ominously, the incidence of death in childbirth did not fall and during the 1930s even rose slightly.[7] Politicians, members of the medical professions, civil servants in the welfare services (many of whom were doctors) and voluntary workers were all involved in child and maternal welfare work, but the scope of these services was limited by the belief that the family should be subject to minimal outside interference, and most of these health officials shared the contemporary belief in the overwhelming importance of maternal responsibility.

Even before the First World War, however, some feminists and socialists – such as the Fabian Society's women's group in the 1890s – had realised the importance of a level of income sufficient for basic food, clothing and warmth in the upbringing of infants and children.[8] In the 1920s and 1930s, women like Eleanor Rathbone pressed for the payment of a Maternal or Family Allowance to cover the full cost of child care. She demonstrated that the average family was not composed of a man with a dependent wife and the three children, but that many children were still in large families with insufficient income while many men had few or no dependants despite being paid a full man's wage.[9] However, family allowances were only introduced in the 1940s as part of the general welfare system. They did not apply to the first child and the amount did not cover the full cost of bringing up a child. The Trade Unions, and following them the Labour Party, were opposed to such a scheme on the grounds that it weakened men's bargaining position based on a 'family wage'.

The suggestion of a Family Allowance for housewives was not the only way that assumptions about women's needs and conditions were challenged. During the closing years of the nineteenth century and the early decades of the twentieth, a substantial number of women attempted to achieve a wide range of social, economic and political rights. After nearly 50 years of pressure on Parliament with no result, the demand for women's suffrage became more militant. In the ten years before the War, many feminists began to want the vote for women as a means to legal and economic reform. Political representation was seen as a necessary first step towards improving the position of women of all classes at home and at work. Women's struggle to gain the vote is well documented by historians; less well known, perhaps is that many women were also engaged in a fight to improve their economic and social conditions. These women, mainly middle class in origin, banded together in societies which sought not only to overcome inequalities in the lives of working-class women but also to gain a public role for themselves as educated women, a role long denied by social tradition and the political system.

By the late 1880s, the revival of the socialist movement in Britain and the 'New Unionism' of unskilled workers, provided a forum for feminist activity. Through involvement with the new unions, many middle-class women were brought into contact with working-class women and girls. One product of the radical environment of London in the late 19th century was the Womens Industrial Council, founded in 1894, which became a centre for feminist commitment in the early twentieth century. Its members formed a pressure group to influence public opinion and overcome 'mass indifference' to women's interests through the method of social reform. The solution the WIC offered to the low wages and poor working conditions faced by many working class women was proper technical education for working class girls to prepare them for entering the labour market and getting a decent wage. However, they also called for increased wages for men so that women would not have to work at least while they had young children. It is clear from the view of the WIC that these social reformers did not radically diverge from prevailing ideas about the role of women. They saw childcare as primarily the responsibility of women and were putting forward ideas for reform consistent with the notion of the family wage. However, they also carried out exhaustive research into the position of women workers which revealed low levels of pay and poor working conditions which had hitherto been hidden.[10]

One reason for these conditions was the concentration of women in only a few occupations, so that the market for their labour was always overstocked (see Figures 1.1 and 1.2). Only a narrow range

Figure 1.1   *Representation of women in different occupational groups, 1911*

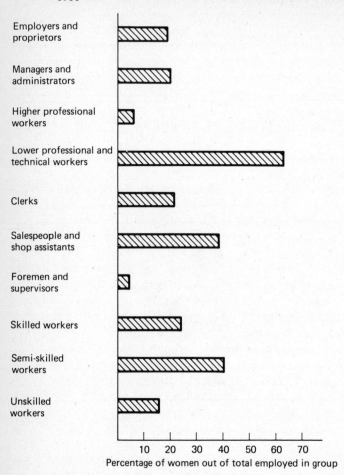

Source: Adapted from C. Makin, 'Sexual Divisions Within the Labour Force: Occupational Segregation', *Department of Employment Gazette*, November 1978, p. 1267.

of jobs was considered suitable for girls and women, mainly connected to their home tasks and not in competition with men's skilled, prestigious, highly paid work. These features were as true among manual as among non-manual workers. In the early twentieth century, the expectation of what work even within this

Figure 1.2 *Proportion of total number of women workers employed in different occupations, 1911*

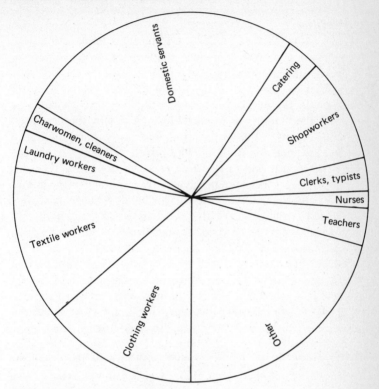

Source: Alison Scott, 'Industrialisation, Gender Segregation and Stratification Theory', in R. Crompton and M. Mann, *Gender and Stratification* (Cambridge: Polity Press) 1986.

range, a woman would do, depended to a large extent on the family she had been born into.

At the highest levels of society the aristocracy and gentry cultivated the amateur ideal. Many men and all women thought it demeaning to work for an income. Their honorific life-style depended on wealth in land and investments. Upper class women's primary task was to set the tone for 'Society', to see and be seen, to show that their family moved in the highest circles and to run their large establishments for the dinners and entertainments which proved their position. Mothers prepared their daughters to 'come out' into Society in their late teens in order to make the best marriage. Girls were trained in accomplishments that had no direct use: languages, music, water colour painting and fancy needlework and dancing.

Upper middle-class professional and business families followed this model whenever they could. If a girl wanted to do something more serious, philanthropy and charity work were her only alternative. This could be Sunday school teaching, visiting the poor or occasionally rescue work among prostitutes. Cottage visiting by the lady of the manor was replaced in the cities by the organised charity movement of the late nineteenth century as an attempt to reproduce the personal relationships which had been lost in the urban environment and to reaffirm bonds of deference. For this alone, the truly genteel woman might leave her home or the homes of relatives and friends. Any activity which paid a salary, however, was regarded as a slur on her father, husband or brother's honour in being able (or willing) to provide for her. Both social standing and femininity were incompatible with paid work.

Although this volume is mainly concerned with middle and working-class women lower down the social scale, the influence of this ideal of the English lady was profound. Women who had been brought up to believe that working for a living was socially shameful, but who had been left with almost no financial resources, deprived themselves almost to the point of starvation before they would attempt to work for money and tarnish their genteel feminity. Those who had worked and whose family fortunes rose, withdrew from paid work to concentrate on domestic and social rituals. Given this constellation, paid work always carried negative overtones for women. There was little career structure even in the few middle-class female occupations like teaching and few alternatives to living in a family, for girls also risked their reputation if they went into lodgings or lived on their own. One of the most important changes instituted by feminists taking up and helping to create new opportunities in the late nineteenth century, had been the creation of girls' boarding schools, colleges, nursing sisterhoods and settlement houses where women might live apart from their families, an alternative way of life for a small minority of single women.[11]

In the mid-nineteenth century, the only option for a middle-class woman to earn money without great loss of status was to become a governess. Governesses were in an ambiguous position within the household. Neither part of the family, nor one of the servants, they were often shunned by both and existed on meagre pay in an overcrowded field of employment.[12] By the 1890s, a change had taken place in employment opportunities for middle-class women.[13] When elementary school became compulsory in the 1880s, a professional body of elementary school teachers working in publicity supported schools emerged. After the Education Act of 1902, secondary education expanded and more secondary teachers were needed. Nevertheless, the teaching of younger children, with its overtones of the maternal role, remained the largest source of employment for women (see the chapter by Widdowson). In the mid-nineteenth century, aside from their notions of ladyhood, middle-class girls had been shocked by the idea of becoming nurses because of the conditions of the time, when paid nurses did only routine and menial chores. With the reform of the hospitals in the late nineteenth century, nursing became a more respectable occupation and the demand for trained nurses grew.

There was also an increase in the number of women employed in shops. This was largely because of the growth of the retail trade which paralleled the contemporary trend in industry towards large-scale organisation. The quantity and variety of goods available burgeoned, which led to a massive expansion of the retail trades and the decline of the small independent shop. These businesses, often family run where women helped informally, were replaced by large units with shop assistants whose unskilled status opened the position to women. The occupation involved long hours, often living above the shop, pay was low and union organisation was difficult. The biggest expansion of all for middle-class women was in the clerical sector (see chapter by Davy). In the mid-nineteenth century the typical business was small-scale and clerks were drawn from middle-class men, many in training for management. Women clerks were then unknown, but in the late nineteenth century, clerical work was affected by a revolution in industry and commerce. The growth in the size of companies led to an increase in clerical work. The fact that many middle-class women were now better educated and the invention of the typewriter jointly led to the growing demand for clerical labour being met by the employment of women. Between 1861 and 1911 the number of women clerks increased 400 times. This work was thought to be especially suitable for women since offices were clean, women were unlikely to mix with unsuitable men and the typewriter was a relatively simple machine, said to resemble a piano. All the above jobs represented new opportunities for single middle-class women. Many of the occupations operated either a formal or informal marriage bar. Women were expected and indeed themselves expected to leave work on marriage, and work was seen as a temporary phase in their life cycle between school and marriage (see the chapter by Sanderson).

If our 'girl of the period' had been born to a working-class family, her expectations and experience of work would have been rather different. There were roughly three groups of women within the working class in the early twentieth century. Among the most prosperous were the wives or daughters of artisans, printers, bookbinders, hatters and the new skilled working class like engineers. They often lived in the suburbs, married late, had smaller families and a lifestyle which resembled that of the lower middle class. Their daughters may have entered the expanding occupations described above. At the other extreme were the poor representing about one quarter of the urban working class and even more of rural labourers who had larger families and often lived on the margin of subsistence. In the middle were the bulk of the factory labour-force.

The generation of the mothers of the young women considered here, was born in the 1860s and 1870s. They were wage earners from an early age, starting with small casual jobs before and after school. By the age of about 12 they would be regularly working until their marriage in their middle-twenties. As married women, they contributed to the family's welfare by a combination of shrewd shopping and housekeeping, gaining credit at local shops and doing reciprocal favours for neighbours and relatives as well as now and again working for money. For this they undertook the usual casual jobs such as cleaning, childminding, keeping lodgers, taking in washing and various forms of homework. A few, who specialised in assisting at childbirth, home nursing and laying out the dead, were known locally as 'handy women'. The greatest pressure to earn came when the children were small and the husband/father's wage had to be stretched to the utmost.

This was sometimes made worse by the operation of the household economy. In most areas, the custom was for the husband to 'tip up' their weekly wage to the mother who would give back pocket money ('spence' in the north). The sum he gave her would become 'the housekeeping' which had to cover all expenses of rent, food, clothing and household equipment plus any treats for the children or herself she could manage. Since all budgeting was turned over to the woman, men did not always appreciate the rise in expense when more children were born or when prices moved up, leaving the housewife to cope with the difference. The grinding double burden of managing household tasks, care of young children and extra earning, eased when the oldest children were able to earn. Then many of these women thankfully gave up paid employment. As we shall see, while the general outlines of this picture remained the same, for the generation we look at, there were important differences in the timing and extent of involvement in paid labour.

In all periods, widows and deserted wives were particularly vulnerable and might find themselves suddenly faced with the task of supporting a young family but with only the usual low paid unskilled women's jobs open to them. In the north of England there was a stronger tradition of married women working in the textile mills, potteries and clothing factories. In the countryside, for all women, domestic service and some part-time field work remained the only two options until after the Second World War. In the south, the alternatives were, by and large, factory work or domestic service, or one of the needle trades, especially in London. In all these areas, women's wages were based on the assumption that she was a supplementary earner. In manufacturing, women generally earned only about half the average weekly earnings of men. Non-manual women workers generally earned a higher percentage of the average male earnings, women shop assistants earning about two-thirds as much as men in 1900. In teaching, the ratio between men and women's salaries was set at 4:5 in 1919. Women clerks, however, received on average less than half of what their male counterparts earned in 1914, while nurses earned little more than domestic servants.[14]

It may be asked why women did not challenge their disadvantaged position in the workforce by joining existing trade unions or, if this was not possible, forming new ones. The reasons they did not, on the whole, do so are complicated and lay in their position in both the workforce and the family. For one thing, in each industry women seldom formed more than a section of semi-skilled or unskilled workers among whom trade unionism was late to develop.

Thus, the problem of women in these trades does not only refer to their sex but was part of the larger problem of organising semi-skilled or unskilled workers. Secondly, low wages meant it was difficult for women to pay union subscriptions. Thirdly, the attitude of male trade unionists made unionism not very attractive among women workers. A union-backed policy of the barred door for women was consistent with prevailing assumptions that women's work was marginal to their own and their families' needs. There was also antagonism on the part of employers who saw attempts to persuade women to join trade unions as an attack on their cheap and docile labour force. Lastly, women themselves often saw their work as temporary and peripheral and so were reluctant to take the time and energy to improve their wages and conditions.[15]

The first attempt at a national trade union for women workers was in 1873 when Emma Paterson formed the Women's Protective and Provident League with the aim of establishing unions in every trade in which women worked. By 1889 it had become the Women's Trade Union League and in 1906 Mary MacArthur became secretary and amalgamated most of the small unions founded by the League into a general labour union, the National Federation of Women Workers. Membership of the NFWW grew from 2000 at the end of its first year to 20 000 in 1914, and women's trade union membership rose during the War only to fall back in the lean years of the inter-war depression (see chapter by Bornat).

Women had been the subject of protective legislation since the 1840s. Their hours and conditions of work were regulated by successive Factory Acts and, in this respect, they were treated in a similar way to children, part of a civil status assigned to those who were not independent agents. Factory and workshop legislation was gradually extended until by 1891 the Factory Acts, at least on paper, covered smaller workshops, laundries and docks. Many employers did little more than comply with the bare regulations while enforcement and supervision of conditions was especially difficult in smaller establishments. Under the Factory Act of 1901, women were forbidden to work at night in any industry. The first attempt to regulate wages of women workers was the Trade Boards Act of 1909 which set up the machinery for Wages Boards to set a minimum wage in four of the lowest-paid industries: chainmaking, cardboard-box making, lacemaking and ready-made tailoring. Although, in the long term the Act was unsuccessful in preventing the 'sweating' of women workers, in the short term it did ameliorate the worst effects of low pay in those industries. It was extended in 1919 to apply to more industries and formed the basis for the Wages Councils.[16]

However, the main work experience of girls and women was completely untouched by state intervention since it was carried out in private homes. By the end of the 19th century, domestic service was by far the largest single occupation for women and girls. In the last quarter of the century, almost 1 400 000 women were in service. On the whole, they were young for service tended to be a 'life-cycle' stage between schooling and marriage. Just under half of all servants were under age 20 and at this time almost one girl in three aged 15–20 was working as a servant of some kind. In 1900, residential domestic service, that is living in the home of the employer, accounted for almost 40 per cent of all working women and girls.

Mothers taught daughters domestic skills and often girls helped in their own homes or those of relatives and neighbours. They took care of younger children, watched fires, did simple cooking, made beds, helped hang out clothes, iron and mend; the tasks getting heavier and more complicated as they got older. Mothers directed their girls into service and coached them into household routines, a discipline and expectation reinforced by school teachers.[17] The experience of service could vary greatly depending on the location, size, resources and personality of the employing family. It ranged from grinding toil and/or neglect to being accepted as part of a family, although this, too, could lead to problems when it came to pay wages or allow time off. Sexual exploitation of maids by master, sons and visitors to the family was not uncommon.

Not all mothers were keen to see their daughters go into service. Much depended on their own experience, their notions of respectability and other opportunities available in the area. The fact that so many women had been servants had a profound effect on their own family life and the way they brought up their children, whether they rejected and resented their time in service or admired and tried to emulate it. One woman who had become a nursemaid herself, recalled the effect of her mother's time as nursemaid and lady's maid in a large household, the elite of the servant world: 'My father was a Conservative (manager of a grocery shop) and because her gentleman was a Liberal, she thought he was right so he was a

Liberal.' Although her mother often had to 'go short' of food and other things herself, she taught her children table manners and 'brought us up like the nursery' including putting food on the table in serving dishes. She kept them from playing with other children and they were not allowed to get dirty when they played. This woman felt she was middle class 'because we were brought up nicely.'[18] Yet paradoxically, women who had spent their life before marriage in the comparative isolation of domestic service had less access to information about contraception and abortion than women who had worked with others, including married women, in factories and mills. As a result, they tended to have larger families, so that it became more difficult to reach the higher standard of living to which they aspired.[19]

By the inter-war period, conditions surrounding service were changing. The war itself had seen 400 000 women and girls leave service for other jobs, many in munitions plants with totally different types of work, the company of others and higher wages. Not all went back after the war was over. The expectation of some leisure time for themselves, particularly to go dancing, to the cinema and take part in the now more time-consuming type of courtship, made the restrictions of service more unpopular than ever. Higher standards of education and above all, the growth of retail sales and office work, made service increasingly look like the place where the less bright and ambitious were left. Even institutions for orphans like Dr Barnardo's began to allow a tiny number of their brightest girls to train for other occupations than the ubiquitous domestic service which had previously been the fate of all. While the depressed state of the economy in Scotland, Wales and the North, or remote rural areas like Norfolk, still drove girls away from home into residential service, urban girls and women were increasingly seeking day work as chars, in laundries or child minding. This did not tie them so closely and they still received a mid-day meal. Employers, too, valued privacy and less formality. Wartime inflation had reduced some of the very large households employing numbers of servants. In any case, the decline in the number of middle class children in each family had reduced the size of the nursery to two or three so that extra hands and feet around the clock were less necessary. Day work was particularly attractive to older married women. Although in the 1930s there were still over a million in service, fewer and fewer of them were living in and they were older. Younger women were seeking other opportunities and domestic service, with its increasingly low status, was an aging occupation. The Second World War, with conscription of women, was the final blow. Only households of key personnel like doctors and farmers were, officially at least, allowed to keep servants.

Domestic service emphasised the same skills, but also similar relationships, as those in the family. As a servant the girl or young woman prepared meals, cleaned, cooked and looked after children. Ideally she studied the personal tastes of the people in the family, was pleasant and helpful, on call at all times. Some of the greatest struggles were over just these questions of personal subordination and autonomy. In the inter-war period more and more servants refused to wear caps, the badge of their subordinate position. Young servants defied bans on singing in the kitchen and, above all, they began to demand more set time off, time of their own. As one maid said: 'You always feel you are attached to the end of a bell.' These characteristics were specific to domestic service. In law and in the welfare system, domestic and personal servants (male or female) were not considered as being covered by a normal labour contract. They had no part in pension schemes and their rights to unemployment benefits were constantly questioned.[20] When the bulk of the young female population left service for white collar work, light engineering or even service occupations in hospitals, schools and other parts of the post-war welfare state, they were not just changing occupations but moving more clearly into the world of wage work.

*   *   *

The inter war years are popularly remembered as a time of depression and indeed there are good reasons for this. Umemployment mounted from the end of 1920 and during the two following decades significant numbers of people suffered long-term unemployment. The old basic industries of the pre-war years – coal, engineering, shipbuilding and textiles – declined bringing mass unemployment to industrial towns in South Wales and the north of England. By the late 1930s Britain was split by a new kind of social, economic and geographical division. Those who were unemployed experienced poverty, though a poverty with different causes and often among different people to that of the pre-war years. But this is not the whole picture. The majority of those who were in work, experienced rising real incomes and living standards. For from the mid-1920s, new industries had begun to develop and old ones to diversify with new methods of production. Electricity, chemicals, domestic appliances, motor-cars, cycles and aircraft were growing industries. New iron and steel products and new textiles such as rayon were made by the old industries, and the formal service sector also grew fast. However, many of the expanding industries used smaller machinery than those in decline, employing a higher proportion of women and concentrated in the Midlands and south.

Government committees investigating women's labour at the end of the Great War envisaged that, while women's employment would expand, they would be confined to light, repetitive, unskilled work processes requiring manual dexterity. Employers regarded women's greater output on repetitive work as proof of their unique suitability for the boredom of the assembly line. Thus after the war, the trend towards employing women in these jobs continued. During the 1930s, the number of insured women workers increased faster than that of men. Female unemployment, though hard to measure, appears to have averaged about two-thirds of the male rate during the 1920s and 30s. Expansion of women's work, particularly in the new light industries and offices, served to offset the high rate of unemployment in traditional occupations like textiles. This did not necessarily mean that women took men's jobs. Rather sections of industry employing women expanded. This was especially true of new light engineering industries. Batteries and electric light bulbs, for example, were made by an entirely female labour force.

The inter-war years saw a change in regional variations of women's employment. The growing importance of the new industries meant that large numbers of women were employed in London and the south-east as well as in the traditional areas of the north-west, while in the north and Wales, the proportion of women in employment remained low. The substantial increase in the numbers of women employed during the 1930s, in particular where levels of male unemployment was not high, indicates a change in attitude away from the respectability of the non-working wife towards the desirability of wage-earning. This change was partly brought about by the desire for higher material standards which the new consumer industries were making possible, and women were keen to take up new opportunities in unskilled, semi-skilled and service occupations.

Nevertheless, the female workforce remained divided by both age and marital status. The persistent tendency to regard all women as normally economically dependent on men was bitterly resented by women who remained single; the older women who found it hard to obtain employment. (In 1931, single women comprised 51 per cent of the female workforce aged over 35.) This resentment expressed itself in hostility towards married women who worked.[21] The commonly held view was that married women did not need to work and, if they *chose* to do so, they were taking jobs away from men with families to support and single women who needed to support themselves. Apart from a few feminists, there was little understanding of the way all women were disadvantaged by the more fundamental sexual division of labour.

This, then, was the setting within which girls born in the 1900s lived, worked and grew to adulthood. Their work experience must also be related to their family environment: how many and who were members of that family, who else was in the household, what was their housing, furnishings, food and level of health, their obligations to others, their free time and leisure activities? In addition, the girls of the generation we are looking at often began work just before or during the First World War, an international event which had major, if temporary, effects on women's lives and work experience[22] (see Table 1.1 and Chapter 8).

By the time our young women were born, around 1900, the chances of early death had been falling but were still unevenly spread between town and country, between age groups and especially between occupations. Those in non-manual jobs could expect to live longer than, say, miners or dockers and so could their wives. Such high mortality was not just due to occupation but also the standard of living and, in Edwardian Britain, there were marked differences among classes in, for example, diet. Among women, deaths in childbirth were high in the nineteenth century, 5 per 1000 births, and they remained so into the 1930s, only gradually falling to 0.5 per 1000 by the 1950s. Differences between girls and boys also varied in childhood. In the nineteenth century more girls than boys died in their teens. They were especially susceptible to tuberculosis, one of the big killers, as well as to diseases connected with poor nutrition. It is believed that the privileged position of the male

Table 1.1   *Changes in women's work during World War 1: 1914–1918*

Numbers of women employed, July 1914–July 1918

Occupations	In July 1914	In July 1918	In July 1918, over (+) or under (−) Numbers in July 1914
On their own account or as employers	430 000	470 000	+40 000
In industry	2 178 600	2 970 600	+792 000
In domestic service	1 658 000	1 258 000	−400 000
In commerce, etc	505 500	934 500	+429 000
In national and local Government including education	262 200	460 200	+198 000
In agriculture	190 000	228 000	+38 000
In employment in hotels, public houses, theatres, etc	181 000	220 000	+39 000
In transport	18 200	117 200	+99 000
In other, including professional employment, and as home workers[1]	542 500	652 500	+110 000
Altogether in occupations	5 966 000	7 311 000	+1 345 000
Not in occupations but over 10 years of age[2]	12 946 000	12 496 000	−450 000
Under 10 years of age	4 809 000	4 731 000	−78 000
Total females	23 721 000	24 538 000	+817 000

[1] Includes the Voluntary Air Detachment nurses and the various naval, military and air organised corps of women (numbering 61 000 in September 1918).
[2] Includes women engaged in domestic work at home and other unpaid work.
Source: International Labour Office, *The War and Women's Employment* (Montreal, 1946).

breadwinner and the low status of girls meant that they were not as well fed as their brothers. Girls also worked more indoors and did home nursing which brought them into closer contact with disease.[23]

Women were also affected by male mortality. Adult men had

somewhat higher death rates than women due to exposure to accidents, the higher incidence of drinking and smoking and the marginal biological weakness of males. When male mortality is combined with the expectation that a man would be several years older than his wife, there was bound to be a shortfall of men able to marry. This imbalance was compounded by emigration. In the early twentieth century, many young men went to the British colonies to take up opportunities created by the Empire. Thus there was a shortage of men to marry at a period which proclaimed marriage as a women's main aim in life. The cultural expectation of a woman's place and the ratio of men to women made this a difficult time for young women and the emphasis on catching and keeping a man is understandable given this atmosphere. Inevitably, there was also a constant pool of widows. In our girls' great-grandmothers' generation, almost one-third of women between 55 and 64 were widowed. Being orphaned and widowed remained a common experience and, together with remaining single, was often associated with poverty for working class women in particular.

In an era only too familiar with death, all mothers were faced with the tragedy of watching some of their babies and young children die, sometimes slowly of wasting diseases, sometimes from sudden fevers and infections. Poorer mothers went through such harrowing experience more often, since such deaths were more common among their ranks, being related to living standards and sanitation. While figures for deaths of older children had begun to decrease in the late nineteenth century, those of infants were still high into the new century, although as time went by more babies were surviving. By the First World War, more people could expect to live through middle age. Women's mortality also improved compared to men and class differences in mortality narrowed. In the late nineteenth century, there had been a 30 year difference on life expectation between the top and bottom class. By the 1930s, for the first time, the possibility of the death of anyone aged 1 to 44 in the immediate circle of family and friends within a one-year period was becoming more remote. Death was slowly becoming something that happened mainly in old age.

Because of the uneven numbers of the sexes, there was a proportion of women who never married. These women lived as lodgers, as servants, with their siblings or as adult children in their parents households. In some families, the youngest daughter would be groomed from childhood to expect to stay at home, unmarried, to take care of elderly parents. If she was lucky, she might then inherit the house or a tenancy although she may have had to give up any paid work. It was estimated that there were at least 300000 middle aged women in this position, some of whom were then left to a poor and isolated old age themselves. By the 1920s, some of these patterns were changing. A higher proportion of men and women between 20 and 30 were marrying, despite the depredations of the War. Thus more people were marrying and younger. Nevertheless, regional and class variations remained. Miners and agricultural labourers had married younger than other groups, the professionals latest of all. In the working class, young age at marriage was associated with areas where work for women was scarce. For example, women tended to marry later in the textile areas of the north.

The most important change in this period was that once married, women had begun to produce fewer children (see Figure 1.3). There was a dramatic fall in the birth rate. In the mid-nineteenth century, our girls' great-grandmothers would have had on average over 6 children and families larger than 10 were common. The numbers of children began to fall in the 1870s when on average women were bearing only half as many as their mothers had done. However at first this was only true for special groups like textile

Figure 1.3   *The decline in family size: average number of children born to couples by year of marriage 1860–1930*

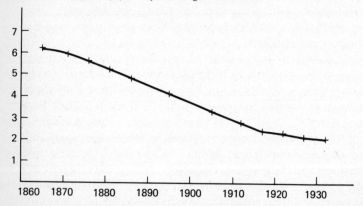

Source: E. A. Wrigley, *Population and History*, 1969.

workers and for most of the middle class. The average number of children in the families of doctors and clergymen fell to four, despite their public stand against contraception. By the inter-war generation, the average for all groups had fallen to just over two. In the twentieth century, working-class family size was falling faster than in the middle class since it had not started the downward trend until several decades later. Thus the gap between the working class large family and the middle class small family would have been widest just before the First World War, the generation of the girls in this book. These changes had made social commentators worried that the wrong people were breeding as there was a common belief in the biological inheritance of intelligence and morality. These fears did, however, draw attention to the importance of maternal health and welfare.

Middle class women, already benefiting from a generally higher standard of living, must have gained a great deal in time, health and energy when released from almost annual pregnancy and nursing. These functions has absorbed their lives from their mid-twenties to mid-forties. By the 1930s, only about 4 to 6 years of the life of an average woman would be so taken up. In inter-war Britain, all groups except labourers and miners in the remote regions, had smaller families on average and those with large numbers of children were beginning to feel odd and somehow irresponsible. The standard of living, housing, travel and education which had developed would have been more difficult if not impossible to attain with an average of even an extra two children in a family. Furthermore, with the decisive fall in infant deaths in the 1920s, it had become clear that fewer pregnancies and births were necessary to raise adult children.

Still another reason for the acceptance of smaller families, was the understanding that children's labour was no longer of as much use to families, not even the type of part-time casual labour so common in the mid-nineteenth century. When schooling became compulsory in the 1880s, mothers lost unpaid domestic help from children, especially daughters. As the economy matured, and the size of enterprises grew, formal wage earning became institutionalised and the grey areas of homeworking and small subsidiary jobs gradually declined. Youngsters were more unequivocally defined as children, particularly by the education system but also in youth clubs and activities they promoted.

From the era of mothers of the girls who are the objects of this study one family in ten had over 11 children, to the time when our subjects' daughters had children, when the 2 child family was normal, was a massive shift. By the mid-1930s family size was so reduced that fewer children were being born than would replace the population and this led to a scare about the decline of the British people. The idea of the small family born when a woman was in her 20s as the expected pattern, was becoming a powerful expectation. The feeling grew that anyone not marrying at the right age and producing her 2.4 children at the right time was more and more an oddity. These strong norms were reinforced by the advances in contraception and medicine which made childbearing seem like a conscious motivation, (family planning) and less like something to be endured. However, contraceptive methods were less than ideal and, in any case, information about family limitation was often witheld from working-class women. Abortion was illegal and risky. the letters written by the members of the Co-operative Women's Guild in the early part of this century, show how appalling the effects of continuous childbirth could be on the health and outlook of working class women.[24]

In spite of the decline of family size, investigations in the inter-war period show how directly working class women were affected by conditions related to the combination of repeated pregnancy and childbirth and the effects of poor housing and diet and overwork. Working class women were liable to minor sickness more than men, partly due to childbirth related factors, but mostly because their waking hours were full of 'small but pressing activities', which made it difficult to protect their health against the results of overwork, lack of fresh air and exercise and irregular, insufficient diet. These women (among whom were some of our girls born in 1900), were subject to debilitating, often painful ailments. Yet when they were questioned for a survey, most said that they generally felt fit and well. This is largely because they had a low expectation of good health and accepted the mental and physical strain which went with bringing up a family. Even if they were to complain, they felt that there was little that could be done about it.[25] Only people in full-time relatively secure and well paid work, mainly men, were eligible for medical insurance and in pre-National Health Service Britain, a married woman's health had low priority in the family budget. It was more important to keep the male breadwinner fit for work and see to the children's well-being. From this point of view, the position of married women had changed little since the nineteenth century.

One effect of the fall in family size, was that children became relatively fewer in the population. British society in the 1880s had been young, children were very much in evidence in the city streets and in middle class households alike. In 1951, the total population had grown by 40 per cent but the absolute number of children was the same as in 1881. The greater stress on the quality of motherhood and healthy children in the inter-war period, was concentrated on the few children in the nuclear family. These changes are clearly illustrated if one thinks of a typical woman widowed in early middle age. In the early period she could be left with as many as 12 children ranging from, say 15 years down to a baby, whereas her counterpart in the latter period would have two children in their late teens and she would probably have been healthier and fitter.

These changes in family structure and size brought the experience of women together across classes and regions, although there were still differences between the best off and the most deprived. Members of all groups now tended to marry younger, had smaller families on average, and could expect their husbands to live longer. Women of all classes and regions had a better chance of most of their children living to adulthood and of seeing their grandchildren born. Women could typically expect a period of lesser domestic demands when their children were grown up and they would be free to take a 'little job'. Despite the small numbers of married women working – about 10 per cent – in the 1930s, the stage was set for the 1950s pattern even without the intervening experience of World War Two. It was in this climate that the generation of young women under study had become middle aged mothers and grandmothers.

During this time, there had also been important changes in the surroundings of peoples' lives including where they might be living. The pull of opportunities had shifted towards the south east with the growing dominance of London and away from the old industrial areas of the north. By 1951, a third of the population lived in the south east, almost a fifth, in and around London. Even in the rest of the country, Britain continued on its way to being one of the most urbanised societies. Just over a third of the population lived in towns of over 100 000 people. Within these towns, the shift was from settled 'urban villages' which had grown up with the second and third generations who had migrated during the nineteenth century, out to the suburbs. Building Societies were growing and set out to woo upper working-class as well as lower middle-class clients. Home ownership began to overtake rentals and became a mark of higher social status. This kind of housing lent itself to creating a home atmosphere. The 'Ideal Home' exhibitions started in the 1920s and projected a similar image to the advertising of the underground and tram companies who had promoted suburban development. *Metroland* projected a cosy picture with 'just Molly and Me, and Baby makes Three' dwelling in 'My Blue Heaven'.

Decent housing had become a major issue for the working class during the First World War, when rents skyrocketed, leading to rent strikes in some cities. After the war, the labour government, under the Addison Act, began to make provision of public housing by local authorities compulsory. Much of this early council housing was in small units at the edge of villages and towns. But by the 1930s, huge housing estates were being built. Yet the rent for these houses was often high and many families found that one wage was not enough so wives tried to contribute and some families went short of food to maintain payments. Meanwhile, many of the older areas, with more depressed industries, did not reach these standards.

Until the Second World War, there were large numbers of people living in rooms or houses without piped water, let alone hot water supplies, or indoor lavatories. Such lack of basic amenities continued to make housework an arduous and time consuming part of women's existence. Members of the Labour Party were particularly concerned with housing, but they, too, had traditional ideas about the lay-out and functions of the home. More radical proposals for communal washing and cooking facilities were unpopular. When the women's section of the Labour Party put out a statement about housing policy. Their members' firm choice was for a small house to themselves with a bit of garden, good large kitchen, a parlour for leisure and mental space, a scullery and cool larder, three airy, light bedrooms, a bathroom upstairs and w.c. inside the house. These ideal homes now housed a full time housewife where the husband was away at work and the children at school all day. They were found in the ribbons of middle-class houses and bungalows along main roads out of the town which could now be reached by car as well as the working-class estates dependent on trains, trams and later buses.

The change in living patterns also shows up in the way households were shrinking in size. Fewer people were now living in more space, from the average experience of day-to-day life with over 6 people under one roof (often in one or two rooms), to the household of under 4 and a substantial minority of single individuals living as a self-contained unit. Although the fall in numbers of children contributed to this change, it was the shedding of lodgers, servants and extra kin – nieces, nephews, grandchildren – which completed this diminution of household size. In this respect, class experience was again growing more alike. Residential domestic service had continued to decline and by the 1950s, working class families were no longer sending their daughters to live as servants in middle class homes and no longer were middle-class children growing up with servants in the house. Middle-class women now had to do much more of their own housework and childcare.

The family-centred culture of the inter-war period was possible because of the rise in the standard of living for those in work. Food was relatively cheap, there was more of it and it was more varied. Better quality clothing, much of it mass produced rather than hand-me-downs from the middle class, gave working people more choice and there was inexpensive furniture which could be bought on hire purchase. The housewife had become important as a consumer of these new goods, as well as guardian of the family's health and she was bombarded by advertisers and experts in carrying out these roles. The women's magazines which flourished in this period played a part, often supported by advertisements for the new products. Listening to the radio together became a family pastime, for, by 1939, three-quarters of households had receivers and the influence of radio was heightened in the Second World War. The cinema began to provide relaxation for married women and films provided a window out of narrow lives although often in the form of Hollywood dreams. By the late 1930s, 40 per cent of the population were going to the pictures at least once a week and the most devoted attenders were women.

On new estates, physical conditions were better than in older inner city areas, but isolation was greater as women were cut off from the traditional sources of information and support from kin and neighbours they used to have in the street or village community. Middle-class women, now with less servant help in the house, also turned inward to an intense family life. There was a new emphasis on marriage which now recognised women's need for sexual fulfilment. Medical discoveries about the nature of reproduction had released more information while psychological ideas were filtering to the public. These made it seem important that the sexual side of marriage ensured companionship while prostitution declined. For one thing, it was feared that women now had so many fewer children that they might get restless if marriage was not made more attractive. There had also been a swing away from the seemingly sexless schoolteacher spinster image. In the nineteenth century, the single life dedicated to others could seem an attractive alternative to stifling Victorian marriage, but now it appeared old-fashioned. The post-war fashions showing off women's figure as free, young and slim with short hair and short skirts, the wearing of cosmetics, smoking in public, the vogue for dancing, were all part of the new image. The shocked public discussion of lesbianism with the publication of Radclyffe Hall's novel, *The Well of Loneliness* in 1928, also made single women's friendships seem more suspect, even abnormal.

Girls born in the 1890s and 1900s had spent their youth living at home under the watchful eye of parents, relatives and neighbours. In the working class, they began their courting by strolling on Saturday nights with their girl friends in the local 'Monkey Parade' of boys and girls, in a street or square by tradition set aside for youthful promenades. When they paired off with a young man, it was to take walks together and have tea at each others' homes, crowded with parents, brothers and sisters. The war broke some taboos which had restricted young women's freedom of movement, particularly in the middle class where Edwardian daughters had led exceptionally protected lives and entered marriage with almost no knowledge of sex, finances, of indeed, matters outside family and home entertainments. Now girls from a range of backgrounds went to the local Palais de Dance or socials put on by churches and clubs. They regularly visited the cinema, a welcome, warm, dark refuge for courting couples. The dozen years between leaving school and getting married may have shrunk to 5 or 6, but there were now more attractions for the girl to spend money on and places to go where clothes could be shown off. Work, by contrast, usually remained a dreary routine, an interval in which to help parents with family support but primarily en route to a trousseau, marriage and a home of her own.

*   *   *

What was the future of our young women born in 1900? What of their daughters probably born in the 1920s and their grand-daughters born into the brave new world of the post-War Welfare State? Our women were to face another World War in 1939, when they were in middle age. By July, 1941 the shortage of manpower was becoming general and all people of both sexes – including girls of 18 to women of 60 – were obliged to undertake some form of National Service. Women were to be conscripted for the first time although only unmarried women between 20 and 30 were called up for the armed services. Others had the choice between the auxiliary services and important jobs in industry.[26]

In mid 1943 the proportion of the nation's women between 15 and 60 who were in the forces, munition work and essential industries was about to double that in 1918 and many more were in part-time employment. By that time it was almost impossible for a woman under 40 to avoid war work, unless she had children under 14 living at home or exceptionally other heavy family responsibilities. In the lighter engineering industries, substitution of women for men was as often as high as 80 per cent. There were around 300 000 women in the explosives and chemical industries, about one and a half million in the engineering and metal industries and women also worked as bus conductresses, in aircraft factories, in the Women's Land Army, as railway porters and as welders in shipyards. There was, however no question of equal pay for equal work. Women in the metal and engineering trades earned on average £3.10s a week compared with £7 for men. There were increased and unprecedent numbers of residential nurseries provided during the war to encourage mothers to enter the workforce, a reversal of pre-war policy. Mothers of young children however, showed little enthusiasm for waged work unless made necessary by the death or absence of the breadwinner. The problems of shopping and running a home in wartime while working long hours also deterred many women from paid employment. They received little official assistance in solving these problems which were made worse by the rationing system which meant registration at a specific shop. On the other hand, general health was improved by rationing because everyone was guaranteed a minimum amount of good quality food and for the first time special supplies were given to young children, and pregnant and nursing mothers.

In the post-war period, the revolution in the production of small scale consumer durable goods had affected women most of all by creating or expanding opportunities for their employment. It was also widely believed that the installation of hoovers, refrigerators, and electric washing machines had given equality to housewives, despite the fact that these aids were only available to the minority of middle-class households that could afford them and who were, in any case, losing the help of domestic servants. These beliefs were of a piece with the anxiety about the family in the post-war period. The welfare state was intended both to ease the lot of the breadwinner and to improve the situation of his dependent wife and children. However there was little thought of basic changes in the division of roles between men and women. Housewifery was to be elevated to a worthwhile career for women of all classes. It was hoped that the more rewarding aspects of childcare and beautification of the home would have higher priority and the drudgery of housework would be reduced. Compared to the 1930s, the Welfare State did go a long way to improving the health, housing conditions and general situation of working class women. For the first time they were well-fed and fit enough to consider the prospect of doing both a paid job and their domestic work as a positive choice.[27] (See Figure 1.4.)

The shortage of labour in certain industries and services after the war – in boots and shoes, clothing, textiles, hospitals, domestic service, transport, for shorthand typists and teachers – meant that women were welcomed as temporary workers in the period of reconstruction, putting Britain back on its feet. Work and marriage were still, however, understood as alternatives. The Royal Commission on Equal Pay (1946) assumed that there were two kinds of women – a wife and mother or a single career woman. But through the 1950s acute labour shortages continued and married women continued to be drawn into waged work. Despite this need, their presence in the labour force was seen as a problem for children, for husbands and for society as a whole. Paid work could most easily be combined with women's domestic responsibilities and secondary status by the solution of part-time work.

The jobs that women do in the labour market today remain akin to the tasks they do inside the home. Despite the fact that over 40 per cent – that is almost half – of the total labour force in Britain is now female, the majority of women work in a narrow range of occupations: the service industries including laundry, catering, teaching, nursing, clerical work and shops. A quarter of employed women work in manufacturing industries and of these half are in

Figure 1.4 *The employment of married women by age groups: 1921–71*

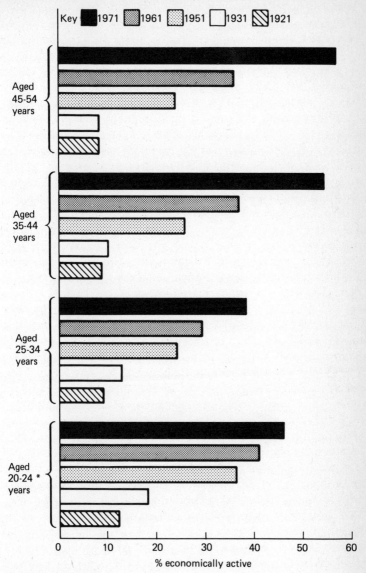

*1931 : 21-24 age range

Source: Censuses of Population. See Appendix 1, Table 2. Department of Employment, Manpower Paper No 9.

only four industries: food and drink manufacture, clothing and footwear, textiles and electrical engineering. 'Womens work' is typically work that requires little training, not much mental initiative and characteristically consists of interruptible short time-span tasks. It is often also described as 'caring' work that promotes the welfare of others rather than the development of the worker herself.[28]

During the 1970s the character of the labour market further changed in ways which have diminished rather than enhanced any prospect of improvement for women. One source of this change has been the spread of micro-technology, another has been the steady rise in unemployment. The silicon chip has been associated with the female sex ever since it made its first major appearance in public (on the tip of a model's nose). Micro-technology is ideally suited to replace many of the unskilled and semi-skilled jobs that are normally done by women. Employers find it easier to introduce new machinery where they do not have to reckon with strong trade unions, and women workers still tend to be poorly unionised.[29]

As the current recession began to take a firmer hold, and the public sector which employs large numbers of women was cut back, calls on women to return to the home became more frequent. The assumption is still that their income is not necessary for the family. However, it is clear that married women's earnings are vital to the maintenance of many families' standard of living, where the income of the wife keeps them above the poverty line. Many women are the sole providers for children or other dependent relatives. Yet it is still not often openly acknowledged that the ideal of the family wage earned by men is incompatible with equal pay for women.[30]

Nothing has happened to disturb deeply the patterns of women's paid work that have prevailed for more than a century, a pattern based on designating a particular function for women in the home and a corresponding function in the labour market. Women's position as low-paid, part-time, intermittent, secondary wage earners has fitted with their role in the home since early in the industrial revolution. Correspondingly their role in the home has been closely related to their position in the labour market. This is as true today as it was when our group of women were youngsters in the early part of this century.

If we compare the experience of the girls born in 1900 with their mothers on the one hand, and with their daughters and granddaughters on the other, we do find some changes. In 1918, women over 30 gained the right to vote and play a part in politics mainly as a reward for their contribution to the war effort. In 1928, all women finally were given the vote and allowed to stand for Parliament, but there are still only about 18 women MPs in the House of Commons in spite of the fact that there is a woman Prime Minister. Standards of health care have improved greatly as have diet and the general standard of living, mainly due to the efforts of the 1945 Labour government and the effects of full employment. As a result, the post-Second World War generation of girls have been taller and healthier than their mothers. Infant and maternal mortality has fallen, although the rate in Britain remains among the highest in Europe. In 1975, after years of campaigning, the Equal Pay Act was finally introduced, followed in 1976 by the Sex Discrimination Act. Under this legislation it is illegal to pay women less than men for the same work or to discriminate against women in employment. But the loopholes in the law are legion and equal pay for equal work has little meaning when men and women do quite different jobs, and while women continue to be crowded into a narrow sector of stereotyped female occupations. Married women's involvement in paid work has risen dramatically, especially for those in middle age, but their work is overwhelmingly part-time with low pay and few benefits. Part-time work fits in with domestic responsibilities, nowadays as likely to be care of elderly parents, as young children. Housework is still seen as women's domain, with some help from husbands if they are lucky. In general, during such a time of recession, 'women's issues' once again take a back seat.

In the late 1950s and 1960s many women were feeling uneasy and guilty as they responded to conflicting messages. On the one hand, there was a stress on the morality as well as need for women to be at home, especially mothers of young children. On the other, there were strong incentives drawing married women back into the work force, from employers who needed them and their own desire for an income to support a better standard of home life, as well as to break the isolation of being at home. Which path should they follow? There were no easy answers. The granddaughters of our subjects were a generation of better educated young women who reached adulthood to find their aims for personal development brought up short against discrimination in the work place and limitations of full time housekeeping with no income of their own.[31] The Women's

Liberation Movement which grew in these decades was partly a response to these dilemmas. It raised questions and provided an alternative analysis of women's relation to both work and family. It is from this analysis that the contributions to this volume have been conceived.

Notes

1. Anna Davin, ' "Mind that you do as you are told": Reading Books for Board School Girls', *Feminist Review*, 3, 1979, p. 20.
2. The legal position of married women rested on the Common Law doctrine of *coverture*. At marriage, a woman lost all legal personality. Her husband covered her legal rights and duties, he was responsible for her debts and torts (minor crimes). She could not make a contract, sue or be sued. In fact, at marriage, a woman 'died a kind of civil death'. The doctrine of coverture was never revoked as a whole but was eroded in piecemeal decisions by judges and Acts of Parliament.
3. Hilary Land, 'The Family Wage', *Feminist Review*, 6, 1980.
4. Charles Booth, *Life and Labour of the People of London, 1892–1902*.
5. Pat Thane, 'Women and the Poor Law', *History Workshop Journal*, 6, Autumn 1978, p. 33.
6. Pat Thane, *The Foundations of the Welfare State*, 1982, p. 174.
7. Jane Lewis, *The Politics of Motherhood: Child and Maternal Welfare in England, 1900–1939*, 1980.
8. They carried out many surveys to show the needs and conditions of working class people. An influential best seller was: Maude Pember Reeves, *Round About a Pound a Week* (1913) 1985. See also: Florence Bell, *At the Works: A Study of a Manufacturing Town* (1913) 198.
9. Eleanor Rathbone, *Family Allowances*, 1949.
10. Ellen Mappen, *Helping Women at Work: the Women's Industrial Council 1889–1914*, 1985.
11. Martha Vicinus, *Independent Women: Work and Community for Single Women: 1850–1920*, 1985.
12. M. Jeanne Peterson, 'The Victorian Governess: Status Incongruence in Family and Society' in M. Vicinus, ed. *Suffer and Be Still: Women in the Victorian Age*, 1980.
13. Lee Holcombe, *Victorian Ladies at Work: Middle Class Working Women in England and Wales 1850–1914*, 1973.
14. Jane Lewis, *Women in England 1870–1950: Sexual Divisions and Social Change*, 1984, p. 166.
15. Barbara Drake, *Women in Trade Unions*, (1921) 1984.
16. Sweating refers to work carried out under unsatisfactory working conditions for very low levels of pay. It usually refers to work done by women employed by sub-contractors who pass on their products to middle men who, in turn, sell them to wholesalers.

17. Pam Taylor, 'Daughters and Mothers – Maids and Mistresses: Domestic Service Between the Wars in John Clarke, Chas Critcher and Richard Johnson, eds, *Working Class Culture: Studies in History and Theory*, 1980.
18. Interview, Essex Oral History Archive, 116.
19. Diana Gittins, *Fair Sex: Family Size and Structure 1900–39*, 1982, p. 42.
20. Leonore Davidoff 'Mastered for Life: Servant and Wife in Victorian and Edwardian England', in *Journal of Social History*, Summer 1974; P. Thane and A. Sutcliffe, eds, *Essays in Social History*, vol. 2, 1986.
21. Jane Lewis, *Women in England*, p. 154.
22. Gail Braybon, 'The Need for Women's Labour in the First World War', in L. Whitlegg *et al. The Changing Experiences of Women*, 1982.
23. Shelia R. Johansson, 'Sex and Death in Victorian England: An Examination of Age-and-Sex Specific Death Rates, 1840–1910', Martha Vicinus, ed., *A Widening Sphere: Changing Roles of Victorian Women*, 1980.
24. Margaret Llewelyn-Davies, ed., *Maternity. Letters from working-women collected by the Women's Co-operative Guild*, (1915), 1978.
25. Margery Spring-Rice, *Working Class Wives*, (1939), 1981.
26. Angus Calder, *The People's War: Britain 1939–1945*, 1969.
27. Elizabeth Wilson, *Only Half-Way to Paradise: Women in Postwar Britain 1945–1968*, 1980.
28. Ann Oakley, *Subject Women*, 1982, p. 133.
29. Anna Coote and Beatrix Campbell, *Sweet Freedom: The Struggle for Women's Liberation*, 1982, p. 69.
30. Jackie West, ed., *Work, Women and the Labour Market*, 1982, p. 3.
31. Liz Heron, ed., *Truth, Dare or Promise: Girls Growing Up in the Fifties*, 1983.

2 'Making Do': Domestic Life Among East Anglian Labourers, 1890–1910

EVE HOSTETTLER

It is generally accepted that for the families of the rural labouring poor at the turn of the century, life was a daily struggle for survival and little more. The level of farm labourers' wages, the condition of many country cottages, the lack of amenities to the countryside such as paved roads, piped water and drains, all indicate a relatively low standard of living for the majority of people in the countryside in comparison with urban areas. It has also been acknowledged that the greatest burden of this struggle for existence fell, not upon the labourer himself, but on his wife, or widow, who every day faced the task of providing her family with the necessities of life out of the meagre income and sparse facilities of the household.

There has been a tendency on the part of both contemporary observers and modern historians to treat the male villager, whether farmer, labourer or craftsman, as the focal point of interest, and to consign the labouring woman and the farmer's wife to the shadowy background,[1] which has resulted in scanty knowledge of the everyday life of the poor country woman at the end of the nineteenth century. An overall impression of grim poverty can be gleaned from a study of the reports of both government enquiries and independent observers, but there is still a veil over the details of domestic life.[2] Oral evidence can go some way towards redressing the balance.

A satisfactory aspect of the oral material collected for this study, was its authenticity which is readily verified by comparison with evidence from written sources such as government enquiries and the investigations of independent observers in the 1900s. For example, respondents' descriptions of accommodation and basic amenities correspond almost exactly to contemporary reports. The Lincolnshire cottage recorded in the 1893 report on the Condition of the Agricultural Labourer is typical throughout the three counties:

> A principal room of say $14 \times 13 \times 8$ (which is larger than the average) with a bedroom of the same dimension over it and a back kitchen of say $14 \times 8 \times 8$, with a bedroom over it. One or other room will have a considerable space taken up with the staircase. The back bedroom will generally have a sloping roof coming sometimes to the floor itself and generally within two or three feet of it.

Mrs Barker's description of the Norfolk Cottage where she spent her childhood gives a more vivid impression of the congested living area provided by such cramped accommodation, but the lay-out of the cottage is similar:

> 'There was one room downstairs, then there was what you call a little back kitchen which you couldn't live in, but you could do the washing up. And the oven used to be in the front room, used to be an oven in the wall, and the copper, for your washing, in the living room – you couldn't call it a front room. There was just one room, you see, and you had to live in it, day in and day out. Two, two bedrooms. There was a washing stand and that – a marble top and a little dressing table – and the bed. That was my parents' bedroom. And ours was the little backbedroom and we just had the table and chest of drawers, well, there wasn't room to swing a cat round, really, let alone anything else, and that's how we used to manage.'

Government Commissioners of the period complained frequently about the ill-health and immorality resulting from the overcrowded bedrooms of the tiny cottages. Mrs Thomas' description of how her mother coped with a growing family illuminates the problem from the inside:

> 'There was – well, one room downstairs and a little kitchen and a pantry, and two little rooms upstairs . . . that *was* awkward – my oldest brother – my grandfather lived a little way up the road, so

he used to sleep up there, my oldest brother. Yes, oh yes, I know, 'cos Mother – there was two beds in the back room, well, when we began to grow up, y'see, my brother used to like to jump into bed with me, see, she altered that! Put a stop to that and we had to go into their room, y'see.

'The girls went into the parents' room, did they?'

Yes, yes – not much room.'

Toilets were usually earth closets, well away from the house and frequently shared with neighbours. Piped water was virtually unknown. While all the evidence concurs on the inadequacies of the water supply, the oral material brings to light a partial solution to the problem favoured by all the women – the collection of rain water in tubs, for household washing. Mrs Nicholson said: 'They never would use a bit of hard water if there was any soft water. That was a terrible thing if they had to use hard water.'

On other aspects of the daily life of the rural poor, the evidence easily bears comparison with the written sources; in *How the Labourer Lives* B. S. Rowntree demonstrated, from a series of interviews conducted in 1912, how family income and the perquisites of a man's job varied from one household to the next; how charity and industry, or lack of either, could materially affect the living standard of a family.[3] These variations also emerge from the oral evidence. Thus in Mrs Bonner's childhood home, the family income was derived from three sources – her father's occasional earnings, her mother's income from taking in washing, and the money which the lodger paid for his keep. Similarly, Mrs Nichols' parents brought up their family on the father's regular wage, his piece work and harvest money which the mother helped to earn, plus her own earnings from nursing and cleaning. Children helped in many families – Mrs Queen went outside in the fields to work with her mother 'as soon as ever we could, about nine or ten, I should think.' Mrs Nixon carried the baskets of linen for her widowed mother who earned ten shillings a week by taking in washing and going out cleaning. Perquisites, though not the abundant fresh eggs, milk and butter of the towndwellers idyll, were all-important: Mrs Bonner's father had a pig and a large garden; Mrs Rampling's father, a shepherd, had besides his 'shilling a week extra' (for being a shepherd), two harvest (lambs and corn) and a bit of land where he grew wheat, as well as a vegetable allotment; Mrs Morris' father kept rabbits and chickens.

There is undoubtedly a wealth of domestic detail in the material. Most impressive, perhaps, is the account of budgeting and household management on the part of the women – the creation of food and clothes out of next to nothing, the use of every conceivable source of material good for the benefit of the family, although such evidence of economy and thrifty housekeeping is surprising in the context of the period.

Mrs Ramplings mother supplied her children with blankets, an item which she could not afford to buy:

'If she wanted say a pair of blankets, say, or a pair of sheets was more – 'cos she didn't buy a lot of blankets, she used to make her own. We used to have an old sack, open an old sack, and then all old stockings, used to sew them on the sack, and then she'd buy a bit of cheap material and cover it – it was an eiderdown! Yes, you get them old wool socks, you know, and you sew them all on an old sack, cover it with a thin bit, pretty bit of material, that used to look nice, you know. 'Bout 6d. for a bit of material, you see.'

Unbleached calico was used to make girl's underwear and socks and stockings were knitted. Providing boots and shoes was of course, as Mrs Queen said, 'a real headache'. They had to come out of the harvest money if there was any left over after paying the rent, and boy's boots were hobnailed to make them last longer. Mrs Queen said, 'Father used to sit up half the night mending shoes', and this home cobbling is mentioned several times in both the oral evidence and other sources.

Food was the major item of expenditure in the weekly budget, and correspondingly the area in which the majority of daily economies and sacrifices had to be made. An exact account of the weekly expenditure cannot be expected in oral material collected after 60 or 70 years, and in any case, there are enough sample budgets from the 1900s to show in detail how close to the poverty line most labouring families lived.[4] The diet which Mrs Baker describes is neither more or less nutritious and filling than the diets quoted in either nineteenth or twentieth century, or extracts recalled by other respondents, but it does include one or two unusual items (such as 'hasty pudding') and demonstrates very clearly how the woman had to solve the problems of supplying food and drink every day to a hungry family:

'A quarter pound of tea had to do us a week, and if we didn't have that – er, when that was done, rather, my mother used to get a crust of bread, put it on the stove and bake it, put it in the teapot, pour some boiling water on it and that was for tea, That had to do – *be* the tea, stand for tea. I mean, if you borrowed from the next-door neighbour, you'd got to pay it back, and you couldn't afford only a quarter pound a week, and therefore, that was no good thinking you'd pay that back out of your quarter pound, or you'd have to go on borrowing again. . . .

My mother used to get the skim milk, what they called skim milk, and of course, that was about a penny a pint. That was from a farm across the way, well, I used to go and get that sometimes – my brother – well, they'd bring that home, my mother'd put it on to boil, she'd get some flour, what they call wholemeal flour, what they make brown bread with, y'know, and she used to boil the milk, mix the flour up with a little cold milk, and when the milk boiled, she'd pour the boiling milk on to it, stir it round and round, put plenty of sugar in – well, I say plenty, what she could spare – anyway, it was sweet, and we used to have that, what they called 'hasty pudding', we used to have that for our breakfast before we went to school.

And for dinner, we used to come home for dinner from school. Sometimes my mother – we used to get a joint once a week, that's all. Well! We couldn't afford no other. Unless of course, she'd been down to the butchers and we'd have some what they used to call scraps, they'd be fat meat dried down in the oven, you see, chopped up in small pieces about so, then the butcher would do them in the oven or in a saucepan or something, boil all the fat out of it, then that was dry, dry chunks of fat meat. We used to call them scraps, you see. Well, my mum used to go down and get some of them and we used to have them. Another time she'd make some potato and onion thickening and cook a dumpling and put a piece of butter in and we had to do with that. . . .

Yes, mother'd make a roly-poly pudding, with jam all in, you know, sometimes she'd make a baked suet pudding, you know, and we'd get that. . . .

My mother would never cook on a Sunday. No! She'd never

cook on a Sunday. Saturday was her day for cooking, and she'd bake her meat Saturday. We'd have dumplings and gravy on Saturday for dinner, Sunday we'd have cold meat, she wouldn't cook a potato even, she was very religious. We'd have bread and something like pickled cabbage.'

Most of the respondents mentioned jam making and pickling as an annual task for their mothers. The frugalities of diet practised by the middle-class suburban housewife, such as they were, were a far cry from those imposed by circumstances on the country woman. Her budgeting was restricted not only by her low income, but also by local shopping facilities.[5] Village shops usually enjoyed a monopoly as far as groceries such as flour, sugar, lard, soap, candles and paraffin were concerned, but other sources of occasional supply took the form of carriers carts, and packmen bringing a variety of goods – such as hardware and haberdashery – and sometimes a fisherman hawking his catch round the village. Allotments and other perquisites added some variety to the diet. But the significantly richer and more varied diet enjoyed by anyone who lived in a farmhouse, when compared to that of the labouring family, demonstrates unequivocally that the labourer's diet, in which flour, potatoes, skim milk and tea play a major role, was a result of low wages rather than of other forms of rural deprivation. That most respondents could outline a day's meal without hesitation suggests that the daily menu varied scarcely at all from week to week, and this is logical in a situation where experimenting with different dishes or new types of food was a risk the mother could not take with her few precious resources; well-tried staples like the hasty pudding described above, or the 'light dumplings' which respondents in Norfolk and Suffolk ate regularly, had to supply the main meals. Few people remembered having anything special for Christmas other than a piece of bacon, a few oranges or an extra large rabbit. One thing which these very restricted diets and very tight budgets serve to underline is the value of every penny, every possibility of acquiring extra food. Such poverty drove men out to dig their allotments by moonlight, women to take babies into the fields whilst they earned a few pennies at stone-picking; took children into the harvest fields to gather the fallen ears of corn, and made the sale of a rabbit skin for one penny a worthwhile proposition.

The evidence on cooking, on the provision of clothes and

household linen and on the general living conditions of the families, all bears witness to the sheer physical burden which the woman bore in her domestic round. Leaving aside the general discomfort of working in the cramped kitchen or living room, taking care not to scald or burn any small children who might be crawling around, the housewife's primitive equipment required constant, exhausting attention if the necessary tasks were to be completed. Consider the work involved in doing the washing, for instance: all the necessary water had to be brought into the house, the copper fire had to be lit and the water heated up, which involved the fetching and carrying of fuel. If no soft water was available, soda had to be dissolved in the water to soften it, the clothes had to be rubbed with hard yellow tablets of soap and boiled in the copper, lifted out dripping wet with a stick or pair of tongs and drained on the upturned wooden lid of the copper before being turned into the tin or wooden tub of cold water for rinsing wrung out or mangled if there was a mangle, then the washing had to be hung outside to dry, or if it was raining, hung indoors over-night. Mrs Nichols' mother had to hang her washing in a garden some distance from the house:

'You had to carry all your linen down there – the washing. And if it rained, or the wind blew, and blew them off the line – and there weren't no mangles then, you see, you couldn't mangle your linen –well, mother hadn't a mangle then – so it would all be just wet, be ever so wet to carry down; course it all had to be wrung by hand.'

Large families created a corresponding volume of washing. Mrs Queen describes her mother's efforts to keep the children clean for school:

'Two winters there was five of us went to school and several winters there was four of us went to school. And we used to have this unbleached – holland, it was – for pinafores very often, and mother used to have to wash and boil and iron, everything, every week, for all of us. I don't know how she did it. Lines and lines of laundry.'

Ironing involved, again, keeping the fire hot, because both flat irons and box irons had to be heated by the fire. Mrs Morris recalled how her mother would get the washing and ironing done during the day:

'When we came home from school, as a rule it was all finished, you see. Yes, they used to get up early and do the washing and get the ironing done; of course, they had to iron with what we call an iron box – that's a box with a handle on, and you put a heater in the fire and made it red hot, and put it in the box and shut the lid and ironed with it till it got cold and in the meantime you'd got another heater in the fire, ready to put in when that was cold. Or if not, they used flat irons – that you stuck in front of the fire and hotted and then ironed with it.'

Mrs Morris said that in the evenings her mother had: 'tons of mending and sewing and all that sort of thing to do'.

The activities of cooking, washing, ironing and bathing centred around the fireplace, which itself required constant attention. The backstock ovens or register stoves with which kitchens or living rooms were equipped needed blackleading and cleaning every day, and then had to be persuaded to burn – not always an easy task according to Mrs Nichols:

'It was built out of brick with a place right at the bottom for the ashes to go down, and a grate higher up where you had to fill it with coal or wood or something, and mother had to heat the oven like that, and that was very temperamental because if the wind blew you had to shut the door, or if it didn't blow you had to open it to let the draught come in. Then it would smoke – like a terror! Sometimes mother used to have to take a mat or a sack or something and beat it right hard on the grate part to let the draught sort of blow the soot away.'

The woman's burden was particularly heavy if on top of all this domestic work she also tried to supplement the family income by earning what she could herself. Mrs Queen's mother, for instance, went stone-picking, singling mangolds and pea-picking, taking the children with her. But she did not neglect her domestic duties, and could only manage to work outside long enough to earn '3d or 4d a day':

'Because, you see, it took a long time to look after us . . . wash and cook for us . . . She always had to be there, when father came in. Poor soul, she used to run, I've known it . . . course couldn't afford a watch, or anything, she used to have to guess the time. She was always glad when she could see men at work in other fields, because she knew they were unharnessing the horses, you see, she knew the time. . . .'

The heavy nature of a woman's work, and the amount of time it consumed, were partly determined by the equipment they used – the backstock fires which needed sturdy iron saucepans to withstand the heat, the flat irons and the wooden or zinc tubs for holding water; and partly by the simple lack of any equipment other than their own two hands. Though some features of domestic life would be common to both country and town, country life was made harder by, for instance, having to carry water into the house, and children having to tramp muddy lanes to school. Like piped water and paved streets, improved household equipment reached the rural housewife long after it had become commonplace in the town. The oral evidence however shows that during the period covered by the interviews new forms of domestic equipment were beginning to make their appearance in the village cottage and kitchen.

The sewing machine, for example, made its first appearance in Britain in the 1850s. Some of the respondents' mothers had a sewing machine, others had not. Mrs Morris recalled how her mother acquired one:

'My mother, I suppose, was the first woman in the village who ever had a sewing machine. Yes, she had a machine. My father and my elder brother were in a, some sort of a club, and for Christmas they bought her a machine.'

The ironing box was considered to be an advance on the flat iron, because the heater went inside so there was less risk of burning the hand on a hot handle. Some women were still managing with flat irons, however. On wash days, wringing out the clothes by hand must have been one of the heaviest jobs and here a mangle was a great advance. The acquisition of a mincer, or grinder, to chop up sausage meat formerly cut by hand, was another step towards lightening the work load. Mrs Bonner's mother chopped all her pig meat by hand on a special wooden block until she got a machine:

'She used to have a square block, wooden block, and she used to have to chop all the meat by hand – there was no sausage machine, you know – and soak the bread. She used to have to chop and chop on this – it was a bit like that box (pointing) only as big again and nearly as high with high sides, you know, that lifted out, but it was a big block, oh, ever so deep, and she used to chop it with a chopping knife. . . .'

Of course, those items of household equipment which represented new developments, unlike items of furniture like beds, chairs and tables, would not be available to the labouring family through inheritance or via the medium of second hand shops and weekly auctions. Village shops would be cautious about stocking anything 'new fangled' and it was probably necessary to save up on a club, or wait until harvest and then make a special trip to the nearest town to make such a purchase. In arriving at the decision to do this, the country woman would be hampered by the pressures of poverty and tradition – just as she would be when considering introducing a new item of food to the family. However, it is apparent from the oral evidence that what can be construed in the context of the times as 'labour saving devices' were slowly beginning to appear in the countryside by the 1900s.

A feature of the oral material which seems to stand in direct contradiction to other sources concerns the traditional domestic skills of beer-making, bread-making and pig-killing – or rather the art of 'putting a pig away' after the killing. There is a continuous complaint, certainly dating from the 1820s and continuing at least up to the middle of the First World War, that the countrywoman lacks these skills. Yet the oral evidence strongly suggests the contrary.

It clearly indicates that a wide range of expertise existed in the districts where respondents grew up. Almost without exception, the respondents' mothers had made bread for the family and in most cases the respondents themselves had learnt to do this:

'She used to have a baking day twice a week, Wednesdays and very often Saturday mornings . . . she used to make two batches of bread in a week . . . she made the dough, she had a great earthern pan and she made the dough and left it to rise during the night . . . shortcakes, what we used to call shortcakes, pastry and currants rolled in and some sugar and cut into squares and that, shortcakes, apple tarts and apple pies, and jam tarts and all those kinds of things, buns and cakes. . . .'

Mrs Nichols: 'We never thought about buying a loaf – no bakers came round.'

Mrs Barker: 'And then my mother used to make bread – she never used to buy baker's bread. She used to make a whole batch of bread. She'd make that overnight and when she got up in the morning, there was a whole bowl of bread – she'd get up at five o'clock the next morning and bake it, and make these little loaves, put a piece of cheese in when they cooked and that was called "toad in the hole". I used to take my father's breakfast, sometimes. A hot loaf! Those were the days, y'know. Beautiful days!'

Dealing with all the meat at pig-killing time was another skilled task which had by no means disappeared from the countryside in the 1900s. This is something which seemed to flourish in Lincolnshire more than in Norfolk and Suffolk and where respondents in Suffolk talked of pig-killing, it was in less elaborate terms than the Lincolnshire respondents. In Suffolk the emphasis was on the bacon, which Mrs Rampling's mother first salted, then sent for curing at Needham Market, then stored in what Mrs Rampling described as 'maltings' and 'malt combs' – a form of waste from maltings which both preserved and flavoured the meat.

Skill with the needle was obviously widespread though not universal – neither Mrs Thomas' mother nor Mrs Nixon's mother were 'much good with the needle'. But as already noted, many women made the family clothes from start to finish, or altered second-hand clothes to fit. Household articles, like rugs, towels and pillowcases, were made at home, and two women mentioned more decorative items such as valances on beds, antimacassars and crocheted chair covers. The respondents seem to have inherited or learnt their own skills from their mothers. Mrs Rampling became expert at the needle at an early age:

'I love hand sewing.'

'Did you do much sewing as a child?'

'Yes. But that was all hand – when I was a child and went to school, I used to spend my evening making these patchwork quilts. I made – my mother had five beds, and I made a quilt to go on every one. . . . Oh, that is a lot of work, yes, that is – I know when I was ill, the doctor come, and he said to my mother: "Oh", he says, "what a lovely patchwork quilt, why I'd like it on my bed, whoever made it?" Mother say, "The one what's laying underneath it!"' '

When Mrs Bonner went into service at 13, she was highly praised for her domestic skills by her mistress. She recalled:

'Well, I got to milk these three cows and I'd half a dozen calves to feed and a good lot of chickens, and I did the lot. And I did all that before I was thirteen. 'Cos I can remember she'd some visitors come one day and they remarked how beautifully clean it was, and she said, yes, she said, "I've a girl here that's better than plenty of girls at twenty. She can milk and do anything and its all done properly." That was me, y'see.'

Oral evidence from such a small number of interviews cannot be conclusive but it certainly suggests that a fresh look should be taken at the question of domestic skills among the rural poor in the nineteenth century, particularly in regard to allegations of ignorance in these matters. From inside the cottage home itself a different point of view emerges, one which does not conceal the hard times, but which also stresses the careful utilisation of slender resources to produce fresh bread from a smokey backstock oven, a shred rug for a bare floor and a patchwork quilt to brighten a cramped back bedroom. If nothing else, the oral material indicates the need for caution in allowing the views of middle class observers to colour our understanding of the lives of rural labouring women.

An aspect of domestic and, incidentally, of village life which the oral evidence illustrated very clearly, and yet which can scarcely be verified or contradicted by written sources, was the variation in living standards and hence in the position of women, within what would be thought of as a homogeneous group. To be the wife or daughter of a farm labourer, or of a small farmer, did not mean the same thing in every case, neither in terms of diet or of a woman's working life. Labourers, in any analysis of village social structure, are generally referred to simply as poor and grouped together without differentiation.

Yet there were degrees of poverty. The poorest household

represented in the interviews was that of Mrs Nixon's mother. As already indicated, she was a widow who took in washing and went out cleaning to keep herself and the three children left at home after the father died – the others having already gone into service. With the death of the father, the cottage and acre or two of land that went with it had to be given up, and Mrs Nixon remembered that they moved twice, the first time to Happisburgh, where: 'We knew when we went in, or mother did, that we couldn't be there very long – the farmer would want it for a man. We stayed there three years.' In this family a typical day's diet might have been:

    Breakfast: bread and milk, or porridge
    Dinner: soup, or a baked potato; rice pudding jam sandwiches
               if dinner was taken to school
    Tea: toast

Asked if she ever had meat, Mrs Nixon replied:

'Christmas. And some weekends. Not often. Sometimes we had some – liver mother would buy sometimes, from the butcher. That's why I don't like meat now.'

The situation of this widow was one of hard work, a poor diet and insecurity of tenure in her cottage; there were no pigs, rabbits or chickens here to supplement the food supply and there was no one to cultivate the 'bit of garden'. In any case Mrs Nixon said that: 'My father's implements were sold, you see, that he had for the land. There was an auction.' Ironically, the death of an older son in the First World War brought a pension of five shillings a week into the house and by that time, Mrs Nixon herself had a job in service locally.

A difference in living standards can be seen between the families of two team-men; here the women and children in the poorer family work harder than those in the better off family, but it is the father's position in relation to his work and his employer which determine the standard of food and accommodation. Mrs Queen, from the poorer family had a father regularly employed at a farm described by her as 'rather a rough lot'.

However, the income was steady and there was a vegetable garden which Mrs Queen's father cultivated. Also, as already noted, her mother went out and did field work whenever she could to supplement the family income and the children helped too. In this family a typical day's diet might include:

Breakfast: bread an butter, or toast with brown sugar tea to drink; father took tea and toast out with him.

Dinner: Bread and jam to take to school Father had 'vegetables, or whatever mother had got' at three o'clock

5.30 Potatoes, perhaps swedes, or green vegetables.

There was no pig here and no chickens. Mrs Queen did not mention rabbits as a regular feature of the diet.

Mrs Morris's father was also a team-man, on a 500 acre farm which was part of the Kimberley estate. The family lived in an estate cottage which 'the Earl of Kimberley had built'. Mrs Morris's father had, besides the garden that went with the cottage, a quarter of an acre of ground for vegetables; in addition, he kept bantams, chickens and rabbits, but not a pig, though there were no restrictions on pig keeping. Her mother did not go out to work unless it was well worth her while:

'I can't remember my mother going out to work until some people came to our village from Wisbech and started a fruit farm . . . and the women in the village used to go to gather them. Then my mother went . . . and sometimes when the picking was good, they really earned more than the husbands.'

In this family the diet is almost luxurious by comparison:

Breakfast: Bread, butter and jam, or new bread buns with butter and cheese. Weak tea to drink.

Dinner: 'Sometimes she made apple pie, sometimes we had a stew. Rabbits were plentiful, you used to often have a rabbit, and dumplings, Norfolk dumplings . . . my father grew enough vegetables to last us all the year round.'

Tea: Just bread and butter; a bloater if the fisherman had been round or an egg (a whole one if it were a bantam's, half a one if it were a chicken's).

In Mrs Morris's family, although the women and children did not have to work as hard as they did in Mrs Queen's family, they enjoyed a better standard of living with one of the daughters, able to take a relatively high status job as a teacher. Although the oral material does not provide a full explanation of the difference, it is possible to identify one or two factors which raised the living standard in Mrs Morris's home and which are absent in Mrs Queen's home: these include generous provision for growing vegetables, facilities for keeping chickens and rabbits, and an employer who took an interest in his workers to the extent of recommending that one of their daughters become a pupil teacher. All these things helped to make life more comfortable for Mrs Morris and her mother than it was for Mrs Queen and her family.

Two interviews which reveal the variations which exist beneath the arbitrary classification of census or trade directory, and which demonstrate with equal clarity that a woman's life chances depended almost entirely on her father's position, are those with the daughters of what would in each case be described as 'a farmer and carrier'.

Mrs Field was one of three sisters who ran the farmhouse and dairy attached to their father's 50-acre farm. He was a widower and as well as being a tenant farmer he operated a small carrying firm, one of several in the village. the day was a full one for the three young women – attending to the milk from the cows (making butter and cheese, taking fresh milk to customers in the village), collecting orders from the village shops for the carrier's cart, baking bread twice a week, doing the family wash, keeping the house clean, and cooking substantial meals – there were six brothers and at one time, according to Mrs Fell the whole family lived at home and worked on the farm or in the carrying business. The father was sometimes in poor health and had to be nursed and they also made clothes for all the family. The sisters helped with the livestock too: 'We used to rear all our own chickens and we used to feed the calves, the baby calves; and we always had pet lambs'. They also went into the harvest fields to make bands for the sheaves of corn. Each day brought a full programme. The food here was very good, 'just good wholesome meals' is how Mrs Fell described them, and this included a mid-day meal of vegetables and potatoes with either bacon, rabbit stew, rabbit pie and Yorkshire pudding, a chicken or a hare in season, followed by a steamed pudding. At tea time: '. . .

they could have a bit of bacon if they wanted it, but we always had plenty of cakes, we used to make all our own cakes, we used to make plum bread and white bread . . .' There was pig-killing, of course, and visitors were always well-fed – with cold ham at tea-time for instance. The difference which free access to the produce of the land makes to a diet is quite clear here, if compared with any of the labouring families.

Marriage marked a turning point and demonstrated clearly how important the girls were to the farm economy. The father, while not actively interfering, did nothing to encourage courting:

'Well, we used to have to do it unbeknown to anyone. Oh, he never wanted any of us girls to get married, not the girls. I don't know why, but we always used to say, in their idea, nobody was good enough for us. And yet, the men, the boys, they – it was quite all right, you see, it come natural. Oh he – when we left home, I shall never forget, when I left home, he sobbed and cried. . . . never forget it as long as I live. It was heart-breaking. I mean, as I say, we all three of us, we had to do our courting behind the scenes, sort of.'

Parent's expectations of their daughters were very different in another, superficially similar household. In Mrs Sharp's childhood home the income also came from a small farm and a carrying business, with the addition of rents from the cottages built on a piece of land bordering the village street. There were four daughters in this family and three sons, but there was no question of the girls soiling their hands with any farm work, and their main duties involved: '. . . light jobs, such as doing the dusting, and making the beds, helping with the cooking, that sort of thing, but not doing the rough work.' For the 'rough work' a general servant and a washerwoman were employed. In this family the girls were neither expected to contribute their labour to the family business, nor to earn their own living elsewhere:

'My sisters, they weren't ever expected to go into any – they – unless they sort of *wished* to, you see. Hetty, Hetty, never left home until she was married, and Amy, of course – Susie didn't or wouldn't have done, after she left boarding school and she was at home, more or less, helping with anything, you know, it was a sort of system, of daughters at home and a girl to do the rough work . . .'

The daughters' suitors in this household were welcomed rather than seen as a potential threat, and the eldest daughter, at least, seems to have occupied herself for part of the time in preparing for marriage. The food in this household was even richer than in Mrs Field's home and it is clear that although the two families would fall into the same category in any analysis of village economic structure, their living standards, and the position of the women in the household, varied considerably.

Perhaps one of the most useful and interesting aspects of these interviews is the way in which they do demonstrate variety in living standards and in the position of women, within sectors of society which in written records would figure as undifferentiated social groups – 'the labouring poor', 'the small farmers' and so on.

The great value of the oral material produced by these interviews is what they reveal about hitherto relatively little studied aspects of rural life. If domestic management is too personal and individual a matter to allow for generalisation, the information on domestic economy contained in the interviews at least begins to cast some light on the relationship between low wages, women's labour and survival in labouring families. In an age when few ready-made goods were on the market and still fewer found their way into poor homes in the countryside, the woman's work and ingenuity were clearly of vital importance in transforming raw materials into a form suitable for consumption. Through the interviews, the women and their families are revealed as both an integrated and yet relatively deprived part of late Victorian and Edwardian society. Like the better-off, they practised careful housekeeping and dressed their daughters in the style of the times, but poverty and rural isolation barred them from many of the advantages of industrialisation and mass production. The memories of the women, or rather of their daughters, provide a fresh insight into cottage life which can be compared with the view of contemporary observers about rural ignorance and slovenly housekeeping. And because they are concerned with women and domestic life, the interviews also reveal a side of village life which is not discernible from the written record – those minute graduations on the social and economic scale which could make a difference between rabbit pie and no meat at all, between domestic service and teaching, between being an unpaid housekeeper-cum-dairy maid and a lady of leisure.

Acknowledgement
The fifteen interviews on which this chapter is based were conducted in Essex, Norfolk, Suffolk and Lincolnshire in 1974 and 1975 with women born between 1890 and 1910. I would like to thank them all for their help.

Notes

1. One example which must stand for many her is P. A. Graham's *The Rural Exodus*, 1892, in which he says: 'As I have wandered in most of the English shires, conversing freely alike with the landlord and tenant, Anglican and Dissenter, the hind at his plough, the ratcatcher working in ditches with ferret and terrier, the Agrarian lecturer, the village atheist, the poacher, the doctor, and land agent, it is my own blame if I have not obtained a tolerably correct notion of the ideas and aspirations of the English villager.' But see also R. Blythe's *Akenfield*, 1972, for a not dissimilar bias.
2. For example: *The Royal Commission on Agriculture*, 1881; *The Report on the Condition of the Agricultural Labourer*, 1893–4; Rider Haggard, *Rural England*, 1902.
3. B. S. Rowntree and May Kendall, *How the Labourer Lives*, 1913.
4. E.g., Rowntree and Kendall; or J. Burnett, *Plenty and Want*, 1968.
5. E. H. Hunt, *Regional Wage Variations in Britain 1850–1914*, 1973.

3 'To Fill the Kids' Tummies': The Lives and Work of Colchester Tailoresses, 1880–1918

BELINDA WESTOVER

Any explanation of women's position in the low-paid sector of the economy cannot be found by reference to the workforce alone. It must take into account women's position in the family both in terms of material and ideological constraints, which vary according to the period in which women are living, to the geographical area in which they live and to the stage in their life cycle. In the tailoring industry, it was common for unmarried women to enter the factories, to leave on marriage and take in homework depending on their family commitments.

The idea that a 'womans place is in the home' and the economic position of women generally in late nineteenth- and early twentieth-century Britain affected the kind of work women did in the tailoring industry and the wages they could expect to earn. Young girls entered the tailoring factories with the expectation that their experience of paid work would be temporary. They expected to marry, to give up work on marriage and be supported by their husbands. Married women who took in homework did so in the face of the assumption that married women did not engage in paid work.

In the context of research into the tailoring industry, the use of interview material has given an added dimension. The interviews were carried out in Colchester where there was a flourishing tailoring industry in the early twentieth century. In the documentary material relating to the tailoring industry, women were treated collectively as a problem which needed to be solved in some way. By talking to individual women who had been tailoresses and who often came from tailoring families, it has been possible to answer some to the questions that could not be answered by reference to other sources. Some of these related to the work situation of tailoresses and some to their family life. In this way it has been possible to make a link between work and home, public and private life, a link which is crucial to a feminist perspective. By using oral material it has also been possible to look at changes in women's lives throughout the period in question.

Informants described in detail what each work process in tailoring actually involved. Differences between factory, workshop and homework are described as well as differences between factories in terms of status and wage levels. Women talked about how they fitted work in with their family commitments and what their husbands and fathers did. They also discussed what alternatives were available to them when they started work and how influential their mothers were in their choice of occupation. They spoke of the lives of their mothers and grandmothers and in what respects their own lives were different. By talking to women who had been tailoresses one could see them as people with individual lives and problems rather than as a 'sweated workforce'.

The organisation of the tailoring industry varied according to the region where it was situated. It employed large numbers of women in the period 1860–1920, and had a rigid sexual division of labour based on differentials of skill and strength. Women's position in the badly paid sectors of the industry remained unchanged with the introduction of machinery. This is important since technological changes are often assumed to have an impact on the sexual division of labour. Tailoring was also one of those industries described as 'sweated' which became a focus of concern from the 1880s onwards.

In this period tailoring changed from a small craft-based industry to mechanised mass production starting with the development of the sewing machine in the 1850s. The sewing machine increased the speed with which goods could be sewn, standardised the products and perhaps created more jobs. The machine did not, however, alter the low rates of pay, nor the fact that most homeworkers were women. Small hand operated sewing machines were incorporated into the traditional pattern of work at home and continued to allow work for money to be fitted in between domestic chores.

By 1900, the tailoring industry was organised around production in factories, workshops and homeworking. In 1901 there were about 150 000 males and 130 000 females employed in the industry.

Women were concentrated in the low paid work processes, mainly machining. Only 1 per cent of women were forewomen and they earned 19s a week whereas 10 per cent of the men were foremen and they earned more than double that amount. Male cutters could earn up to 35s 5d a week, and no women were recorded as cutters on the 1901 census. There were very few women pressers and their earnings were less than half those of the men. The small number of men machinists earned up to 30s 9d a week compared to 13s 5d for women machinists.[1]

Women who began work as girls in the tailoring factories just before and during the First World War could usually remember exactly how much they received when they started as learners, between 1s 6d and 4s 9d a week. Their working day usually began at 8 am and ended at 6 pm and there were no tea breaks until after the First World War.

'I got four shillings a week when I started. That would be when I was fourteen. That would be 1910. 'Course you went straight from school to work in those days . . . I stayed there seven years until I got married. We used to work from 7 in the morning to 7 at night. We had an hour for lunch.'

'Did you have any tea breaks or anything?'

'Oh my dear, No! You could take a bit of food in but you had to have it in between your work . . .'

Usually girls spent their first six months on the learners bench:

'Yes, well, my mother said to me "If they don't put you on a machine, you come home". I said "Alright, Mum", 'cos my Mum was boss, you had to do as you were told in them days. So I went home 'cos they put me on a table cutting off ends. Howsumever, the next day I went back as if nothing had happened 'cos they promised to put me on a machine as soon as there was one empty. And at that time of day, they used to have what they called a 'learners bench' and I had to wait my turn. When that learner had done her six months training they went on another bench and they went on their own time. 'Course that was when they started to earn more money. So in the end I got on the learners bench and I was on that bench for six months at half a crown a week.'

Once the tailoresses were 'on their own time', they earned no money if there was no work available:

> 'You done a year when I was at Leanings – thats where I learned my trade. When you done that you came on your own time; what you earned you took. If you earned five shillings then you took five shillings . . . but they never made your money up, if you had no work you just sat there, you never got no wages made up.'

In discussing the conditions in factories, the general view was that 'we had some good times as well as bad times but they were hard times':

> 'You took it as that was your lot to be out of work in a factory and you didn't think about it. When I married I was glad to get away from it but I was happy there in a sense. I liked the company of the girls and there was always something doing something funny. . . . But the time was long in some of those factories and the heat was shocking. I used to feel sorry for the girls on the presses with the steam pouring out.'

The methods of production in the tailoring industry were far from being standardised in this period. At one end of the scale were the large factories equipped with power driven machinery. The factories employed mainly women, generally speaking in making one part of one garment:

> 'Then the latter part of the time they went on what they called "section work" and one used to make sleeves, one used to do backs and one used to put pockets on.'

However, some women in the smaller factories would learn the trade throughout and their status was better. They recognised that women felt alienated when they only made one part of one garment and never saw the finished product and there was less pride in the work:

> 'Well I was a coat machinist . . . and the only thing I didn't do was put the buttons on and buttonholes and finish round the sleeves. They used to call us the "posh factory" . . . 'course a lot of

factories – some made all the sleeves, some made all backs . . .
but there you were taught the trade right through. That was much
better really.'

'We had to do a year's training 'Cos you know we made the work
right through. . . . We fitted the jackets up and fitted all the
lining in. . . . We didn't cut the coats but we made a coat right
through. Finished. It was a lot better, by making them in parts
you didn't know whose fault it was.'

The factories the two women quoted above worked in were small
and closer in style to workshops because they made bespoke
garments that is those that are individually ordered and fitted as
well as 'specials'. The workshops employed from 5 to 40 workers
and were equipped with hand or treadle machines but had little
other machinery. They were managed by a master tailor who
usually worked side by side with his employees.[2]

At the bottom end of the scale were homeworkers. The employment of homeworkers in the tailoring industry benefited the
employer in several ways. Little capital was needed either to start a
business or carry it on, most of the running costs of rent, heat and
lighting being borne by the workforce. In a seasonal trade the
employer may have found it more profitable to run his factory on a
minimum load and take on homeworkers in busy periods.

Homeworkers were prevalent in those areas of the country where
men's wages were especially low; those districts where casual or
seasonal labour was the usual employment pattern for men; those
areas where there was no alternative employment available to
women and in areas with a marked surplus of women. Women took
in homework only out of economic necessity and because they had
young children or dependant relatives. They were in a poor
bargaining position partly because they were not geographically
mobile. Most of them were married women who were not able to
move about in search of better-paid work. They were also isolated
and working in a labour market where the supply of labour
exceeded the demand.

Like many other craft workers, the tailors wanted to protect their
status as skilled workers and wages which went with this status from
encroachment by women workers who they felt would tend to
reduce wages and de-skill the industry. Women, they believed

should stay in their own sphere and not undercut men's wages. The sexual division of labour in the industry reflects the desire to protect and keep certain jobs for men only. Cutters were usually men as the work was perceived as being too skilled and too heavy for women to undertake. Pressing, similarly, was viewed as men's work as was heavy machining. Apart from foreman, cutters earned the highest wages in the industry. It was clearly a job worth protecting from encroachment by women. Moreover, it was possible to keep cutting a male occupation because comparatively few cutters were required in factories and often only one in workshops and there was not the same necessity when demand increased for a large new supply of labour which could be met by employing women as was the case with machining. Male pressers were not able to protect their jobs from women in the same way as cutters because the factories needed women to become pressers. However, there were far fewer women and they earned well short of half the male rate.

The reasons why there were no women cutters and few pressers was not really because the work was too skilled or too heavy for women to do. In other areas of employment, for example domestic service, women were expected to perform heavy tasks which required both physical strength and stamina. It was because these jobs were scarce that men were able to protect them from encroachment in a way that journeymen tailors failed to do in the early nineteenth century for sewing.

*   *   *

Women then, were concentrated in the lowest paid sector of the industry. The remedy for the low wages and poor working conditions of many workers in the sweated industries in the early twentieth century was seen to lie in two directions. Firstly, it was considered that they should join trade unions or set up their own. Some limited success was achieved in this direction in the years before the First World War. But the organisation of women in the sweated industries like tailoring was highly problematic. They faced opposition from employers, from male Trade Unionists and were hampered by the double responsibility of home and work.

The second solution was seen to lie in minimum wage legislation. The Trade Boards Act of 1909 was an important piece of legislation. It set a minimum hourly wage in four of the sweated industries including tailoring. It was the first time that the government had interfered in the area of wages. This had hitherto been viewed as a matter between employer and employee. In the short term the Act had some effect, it seems to have contributed to an increase in the minimum wage earned by women in the sweated industries and had some small effect on the number joining trade unions. In the long term, it has had almost no effect. In fact, the Trade Boards Act institutionalised and made legal the principal of unequal pay for men and women by setting different minimum rates. The problem is that any measures which seek to ameliorate the condition of women workers by organisation or legislation, that do not take into account the fact that women are not only wage earners but also wives and mothers are doomed to failure.

The First World War caused many structural changes in British society and industry. Assumptions about the work that women were able to do were questioned and prejudices against women in certain jobs were undermined. With the enlistment of male workers from the tailoring industry into the armed forces the question of the replacement of men by female labour was discussed by the employers organisation (the Wholesale Clothing Manufacturers Federation) and the Home Office. The Home Office wanted the employers to agree that any women employed during the war would be asked to leave when the war ended. The employers would not agree to this but said that they would keep their promise to individual employees that they would get their jobs back after the war. There was some pressure from the Trade Unions to get guarantees that no women would replace men unless it was absolutely necessary and that 'dilution' would only last for the duration of the war. Whereas before the war the government had passed legislation aimed at improving the situation of homeworkers during the war government contract work was given out as homework at rates that could not but reduce the women to the position of sweated labour. Women were employed in large numbers in the tailoring industry during the war. In pressing which was mainly done by men before the war and previously considered too heavy for women to do, women were taken on in large numbers in some factories. Many women replaced men in hand cutting, although band-knife cutting was a reserved occupation and few women did this. This clearly demonstrates that describing work as 'heavy' or 'skilled' and therefore for men was a rationalisation and a device for excluding women from scarce and well-paid jobs in tailoring.

Khaki cloth for the army found its way from the direct Government contractors to small towns and villages around the country and it was the unprotected and unorganised women workers who suffered most from this. Khaki was extremely heavy and unpleasant material to work with. Most homeworkers in the villages around Colchester made army clothing of more lightweight materials. But Mrs Crow had an industrial machine:

> 'Of course I got married afterwards and my husband went into the army. Well then I still lived at home with my mother and we had all this military work – khaki. Oh dear and wasn't that a business because it was heavy you know. Well of course, I had a big industrial machine . . . 'course I couldn't do heavy work like that on a small machine . . . had to sit very close 'cos it was a job they wanted done already.'

Many of the informants spoke of the long hours, low wages and arduous work in the tailoring factories in war time. They felt, however, that they were contributing to the war effort in the best way they could by making uniforms and palliasses for the soldiers at the front.

*   *   *

The wages and conditions of tailoresses whether working in factories, workshops or as homeworkers varied according to their geographical location. Colchester had been a tailoring area since the 1850s. The low earnings of tailoresses in Colchester were caused by the general industrial character of the district. In the Colchester area, the men's wages were low. There was a large agricultural population within easy reach of the town and the wives of these agricultural labourers needed to supplement the family income with work of their own. The conditions for men in the area – the lack of alternative employment and low agricultural wages – meant that women were obliged to work for what pay they could get. The intermittent and, generally speaking, low level of trade union activity among men was one of the factors militating against women joining and becoming active in trade unions. Some of the tailoresses in Colchester lived and worked in the town itself. Many of the homeworkers, however, lived in the agricultural villages and the coastal villages where the men were sailors and fishermen.

The Colchester tailoring industry began in a small way in the early nineteenth century. Then, in the 1860s, a succession of London firms began to establish branches in the town to take advantage of the cheap labour available both in the villages and among the fast growing female population of Colchester. With the closure of the silk mills in the early nineteenth century, only domestic service and a small amount of shop work offered alternative employment. It was estimated by the Select Committee of the House of Lords on the Sweating System (1890) that labour was half as cheap in the provinces as in London.

By 1900, 1500 girls were employed in factories in Colchester. This was only a small part of those actually employed in the tailoring industry since most firms set cut-out garments to be made up in the surrounding villages up to a distance of about ten miles. Most were taken by carriers' carts of which there were about sixty running every week between Colchester and places in the vicinity. The finished garments were fetched back by the same means.

There was strong feeling in the local press of the time that tailoring was a sweated industry. The solution to the problem was, predictably, seen to be the organisation of tailoresses into trade unions. This was suggested over and over again with no real results until the First World War, and was based on a lack of insight into the particular problems faced by women workers. Those concerned with improving their position usually tried to organise them on the same basis as male workers, as if the two were equivalent.

There were three basic problems concerned with the organisation of tailoresses in the Colchester area. Firstly, the area was one of low pay for men and of low levels of industrialisation and lack of class consciousness which led to poor organisation among male workers. The second factor was the structure of the tailoring industry in Colchester which was one of small family firms where the women owed or felt they owed a personal loyalty to the employer. Such personal loyalty militated against the formation of solidarity based on common class perceptions. Moreover, the structure of the tailoring industry which was divided into factories, workshops and homeworkers meant a lack of spatial and psychological cohesiveness among its workers. Thirdly, tailoresses had problems that were faced by women generally. The major problem from their point of view was undoubtedly the double responsibility of home and work.

I talked to women who had been tailoresses in Colchester in the early years of the twentieth century about the links between their work and family. I wanted to find out what the alternatives had been for them when they started work, and how important their mothers had been in the choice of employment. I also asked them about attitudes to married women working and about their reasons for taking in homework when they married. Interview material reveals these women as individuals who made rational choices about their lives within the constraints of the options open to them, rather than as a tiresome problem in the male labour force.

In Colchester, the choice for girls starting work in the early 20th century was between domestic service and the tailoring factories. Interview material reveals how they made this choice. Domestic service was often favoured by the girl's mothers because it was seen as more respectable than factory work. They also thought that it would prepare their daughters for married life.

'*I suppose you could've gone into service?*'

'Oh no. I wouln't've liked that. I couldn't've stuck that. . . .'

'I didn't know which [job] to take so my mother said: "you use your fingers with needlework and that".'

'*How old were you then?*'

'Yes, 14.'

But they did not always do as they were told by their mothers:

'My mother said: "If you don't go into service Eth, you'll never know how to do anything." I said: "No, I'm not going to wait on other people's arses for nobody." [laughs] And for me to say that to my mother! I never heard my mother say "arse" in her life. Never!'

Mrs Morris helped her mother do tailoring and she didn't want to go into service either:

'Most of us had got bigger families than they do today. The thing is she [my mother] did the tailoring at home. She used to finish the trousers and I used to sit and put buttons on at night.'

'That's how you started doing tailoring?'

'I suppose it was.'

'What were the opportunities round here if you didn't go into tailoring or service?'

'That or serve in a shop.'

'I suppose there was even less for your mother's generation?'

'Yes. Go into service, that was the recognised thing really. To go into service, young girls when they left school.'

'Did you think about going into service at all?'

'No . . . I couldn't bow and scrape.'

When asked what she could have done if she hadn't gone into tailoring, Mrs Potter had this to say:

'Well, there was nothing else, I thought about. Wherever I went, it'd gotta be tailoring. When I first started, I'd either got to go into the factory or service.'

'You didn't want to go into service?'

'No fear! I didn't want to go into service . . . and men used to serve in the shops even in ladies shops, they never had women in shops until the war broke out, the men had to go and they brought women in. When I was 14 there was no women in shops, all men, selling knickers and all.'

It was easier for these girls to get a job in one of the tailoring factories if they had family connections. This applied particularly to the bespoke tailoring concerns where jobs were scarcer and wages and opportunities better. Mrs Scott's family had all been in the tailoring and she was able to obtain a job with Leanings, a well-regarded bespoke tailor:

'How did you get into tailoring in the first place?'

'Well my grandfather was a tailor and my mother and all my aunts worked in it and so . . . there was nothing really for us to do, we had no option, we were just put to it, I mean when your family . . . well that was just your life, there was nothing else and I suppose we didn't think of anything else, not like today.'

'You didn't think about going into domestic service at all?'

'Oh no, no. 'Course that was the choice wasn't it? My father would've liked us to go into domestic service 'cos his people were in domestic service but my mother's were all in the tailoring line so that's how we got there, we had no choice.'

'Had your grandmother been in tailoring?'

'Yes and my grandfather both did tailoring. That's how it was in the family, I suppose.'

'Was it more difficult to get into skilled work?'

'Yes, it was more difficult to get into Leanings, they wanted to know what you were and where you come from . . .'

'Did your mother used to do tailoring at all?'

'No. All my father's people did . . . in fact my grandmother and my aunt used to work for Turners and that's a few years ago. That's how I come to get there.'

'Going back to when you first started, were there any other choices really?'

'Well I don't really know. I think my mother got me that job and I just went. Well you did, you didn't rebel or anything like they do nowadays.'

Both Mrs Frost and Mrs May had family connections in the tailoring trade:

'My grandmother, my mother's mother was not a tailoress but her husband was. He was a private tailor and my father's sisters were all tailoresses practically every one of them.'

'So you went into tailoring because of your family really?'

'It was born in me I suppose. I was not any good at school at anything else . . . and I always got the top marks in needlework so it must have been born in me. My mother was a tailoress.'

Informants spoke of distinctions between the tailoring factories and workshops in Colchester. The most prestigious and well paid jobs were in the small workshops. These employed between five and fifteen girls under a master tailor. The girls made the garments 'right through'; that is from beginning to end. Jobs in these workshops were difficult to obtain and family connections were crucial. In the tailoring factories, the girls usually only made on part of one garment. This work was perceived by the workshop girls as unskilled 'slop work'. The tailoresses in the factories looked down in their turn on the homeworkers from the villages. They called them 'country bodgers' and said that they often had to undo the work they did and redo it. These perceived status distinctions were caused by and reflected the pay and skill differentials attached to the various jobs. Some of the tailoring factories had a better reputation among the tailoresses than others. Informants tended to support the particular employer they worked for. Those who had worked for several employers ranked them according to wages, working conditions, regularity of work and the attitude of the employer to his workers.

Following the national pattern, most of these girls left work when they got married. The prevailing attitude to married women working depended on the type of work they did. Domestic work was considered suitable as was any form of sewing, especially if it was done in the home. Taking in washing or lodgers were other acceptable possibilities for married women in the period. Factory work for married women was criticised, especially if they had children. The view that married women should not work outside the home is reflected in my interviews.

Most of the women stopped after they were married, although some returned when their children were older. They were asked whether they or their mothers had returned to work after they were married. Most said that married women did not work in those days, even if they then went on to say that their mothers had in fact taken in homework.

'But I never went to work after I married . . . well that was unheard of thing in those days, wives going to work . . . you was looked down upon if you had to go to work, you was looked down upon as if you was poor.'

'Were they all young girls working there?' (*in the workshop*)

They'd all started from school and they worked up . . . some of them you see, they remained old maids. Only us younger ones what got married then left.'

'Did any of them stay on after they were married?'

'No, all left.'

'Did your mother work after she was married?'

'No, I don't know they seemed to think if a woman worked after marriage . . . it was something to be ashamed of. You were looked down, on. You could do it at home and they didn't take too much notice of it . . . like my mother, although she did it at home she never went *out* to work.'

Husbands would accept their wives working at home as long as they didn't work too long hours:

'In fact, I got married and my husband didn't want me to do it any more . . . but he didn't mind me doing the finishing at home.'

'Did you work long hours at home?'

'I pleased myself. My husband wouldn't let me work long hours. If he was here, in the evening time . . . he used to say: "Come on now, its time you left off. . . ." I never used to have no specified time. I'd do it when I thought I would.'

There was also a feeling that things had changed:

'Did you go out to work after you were married?'

'No. I never went out to work after I was married. There wasn't many who did. They used to cry shame on them in them days when they were married if they went to work. They used to say your husband should keep you. 'Course today its different . . .'

It was accepted that women could take in work at home although this often meant working longer hours for less pay.

The worst cases of sweating were found in the home.[3] It is not possible to generalise about the wages and conditions of homeworkers there were different rates for the same work according to the region and employer. Since homeworkers received piece-rates but, when asked, could not remember how many hours they worked a week, it is not possible to work out a weekly rate of pay with any degree of accuracy. They tended to fit in the work with their domestic commitments and if necessary to work into the night during busy periods. This comes across clearly from interview material:

'I used to put the baby to bed at night and I'd sit on my machine here and start about 7 till 10. I used to do the finishing in the morning, in that hour between working and looking after me family, you know.'

Piece work rates paid by the Colchester tailoring firms ranged from 3d for a pair of trousers in the late nineteenth century to two shillings just before the First World War.

'How much do you think you and your mother could earn in an average sort of week?'

'Well . . . if it was two shillings in the old money a pair we used to think that was good. I have made them for eighteen pence.'

'They brought it here by cart and they hired a room, and the women had to take the work in to be passed. The rate for ordinary work was 3d a pair. The person who had the machine had the 3d. She did the machining then she would pass the work onto the people who did the handwork. They had to sew the bands in, do the flies and sew the buttons and the button holes and do the turn-ups and they got half, they got three ha'pence. That was accepted. But the whites was 4d and the people who did those were very special people.'

Each machine would be supplying three or four other women.

'How many pairs of trousers do you think your grandmother used to do a week?'

'Oh well, they would want to do two or three pairs a day.'

Homeworkers in the tailoring industry of Colchester were mainly engaged in plain machining:

'I used to make thirty pairs of trousers a week. They were all cut out ready. 'Course you had to make 'em properly. Sit down at the machine and put them together you might as well say. They used to all the sewing part in the factory, you see.'

'You know it was all cut out by an expert cutter. They only put them together. But they had to know exactly how to do it – it was an art – I shouldn't have been able to do it. The trousers had fly fronts – no zips in those days – and that wasn't easy to do.'

Women who took in tailoring in the villages around Colchester had often helped their mothers as children and started working on a machine as soon as they left school. They were often taught by their mothers although some of them later went into the factory to learn a new skill. Mrs Samuels, a local historian in Great Tey said:

'It was handed down from mother to daughter, you see, the daughter would be at home and she'd see her mother doing it and so it was passed down the generations round here.'

Mrs Crow lived all her life in Aldham and learned tailoring from her mother:

'Well, I was 14 years old the day I had my machine and I started straight away with my mother you see, she learned me. Of course, I was only the girl in the family, three brothers, they didn't want me to go out to work so I did the work at home which was very useful to me afterwards. We never cut no work out ourselves, we had it brought to us already cut out from the factory.'

The women in the coastal villages were responsible for bringing up the children and looking after the home for much of the year while their husbands were away at sea. There were no gadgets to lessen the hard work of keeping the houses, clothes and children clean. Clothes had to be washed by hand, starched and ironed without electric irons. Water had to be fetched from the stream, wells or pumps. Tailoring had to be fitted in whenever possible with other family commitments.

> 'My mother? She always did the tailoring. She used to work for about 4½d a coat. She used to make these corded coats you know, with corded edges.'

> 'I don't know how many dozen she done a week but she was glad of the money – just what little money they earned and . . . she used to sit and work with us all around her you know. There was nine of us 'course the elder ones got up a bit before the little ones came along. My mother did the tailoring all the years that I remember.'

The children used to fetch and carry the tailoring for her:

> 'Mr Jones the carriers cart used to bring it out and sometimes we had to walk to town with a bundle of coats done if mother wanted the money. We used to go and take the coats and walk to Colchester with them. . . . Yes it was an awful long way wasn't it?'

> *'Did you children used to help her in other ways?'*

> 'We used to press the seams and the sleeves . . . when we came home from school.'

Mrs Crow remembered that her mother used to have to walk to Colchester and back with the tailoring on the pram:

> 'Of course before I was big enough to take it on they used to have to take it and walk into Colchester with it on the prams. I remember all of that and from Eight Ash Green to Lexden there wasn't a house nowhere. It was all plain and dark and my mother and Mrs Bailey . . . they trudged along with the prams to take this in . . . and then they'd bring it back, once a week.'

> 'Them days were terrible. After, when I did it they brought the van out, I should never have done that.'

> *'They must've been desperate.'*

'They were hard times then you know.'

Mrs Potter came from a large family in Colchester and the children all helped their mother with the tailoring:

'Before the war did your mother ever take in tailoring at home?'

'Yes! I was born with a needle and cotton in my hand. She used to do the finishing. My Aunt Miriam used to machine the trousers and we kids used to have to go down there and get these and bring 'em back and my mother would put the pockets in and the buttons on. My mother used to say: "Well, its your turn to stop up tonight." That's me. And she said: "You can sort the buttons out for me." I used to sort the buttons out what she was putting on the trousers and then she'd say: "If you get a needle and cotton, you can put some on." Ooh, I'd say, that'd be nice. I thought that was lovely. I thought I was doing her a good turn, well I was really,'

Her mother had twelve babies in 11 years, some of them twins – only six survived. Even when she was confined she did not give up doing the tailoring:

'Well my mother had a lot of babies that I knew nothing about much. Every little while I'd come down and see a baby on the sideboard . . . and there would always be baby's little coffins and she used to be laying in bed and she'd be putting these buttons on the trousers . . . as she lay there.'

Mrs Spratt's mother tried to do tailoring but her eyesight was too bad. Left a widow with three children, she did washing and charring to make ends meet:

'She used to have 24 sheets at a time, different people – 1½d each time it was in them days. She did work hard. She was only 39 when she was left with us three – no help in them days. She used to go to work from 9 till 12 for 9d – go out charring. She used to get up at 5 o'clock in the morning and do some work, washing. Leave off and get to work by 9, come home at once. . . . That was hard work in them days and bad pay.'

Whatever married women earn and for whatever reasons they work, their earnings are described as 'pin money'. It is often considered that they worked to buy luxuries for the family or for themselves. It was suggested by Clementina Black that the women of Rowhedge worked to buy 'pretty clothes for their children or for themselves: a bicycle, a piano.⁴ I discussed the question of 'pin money' with the women from Rowhedge that I interviewed. They believed that the income that the women of Rowhedge received for tailoring was vital to the welfare of their families:

> 'Well she [her grandmother] died in 1924 and she was 81 then and I have often thought to myself that times were jolly bad in those days because there was no money about for one thing and when the men did go to sea, when they were young and fit and when they were yachtsmen there was never very much in the winter you see.

> So that really and truly taking the biggest part of the families in Rowhedge, they were brought up, or helped to be brought up, I should say, by their mothers doing the tailoring at home. . . . That was the only thing that the women *could* do you see. There was no transport to get into Colchester, no buses I mean, they'd got the kids at home and they'd got a machine. . . .'

She felt that employers were well aware of the situation of the women in the coastal villages:

> '*Do you think the employers took advantage of this?*'

> 'Well yes. Well you see the thing was people were glad to do it to earn a living and when things are like that you know, there's always somebody to take advantage of those sort of people.'

> '*I suppose they either did tailoring at home or nothing.*'

> 'No, there was nothing else.'

> '*So they didn't do it for a bit of pocket money?*'

> 'Pocket money! That was pocket money! To fill the kids tummies. No-one worked on the tailoring at home unless it was to fulfil a need. . . . they had to. If the husband lost his job – no dole – no money coming in.'

Agricultural labourers in the villages around Colchester earned very low wages compared with those in other areas of the country. It is clear from interview material that the money the women earned was also essential to the welfare of the families:

> 'Most of the women in Mersea used to do tailoring, jobs for a factory in Colchester. Yes. That's really – it was the women that really kept people alive, kept people going. I remember my mother and my grandmother doing it, doing buttonholes and coats and things like that . . . sweated labour absolutely. My grandfather was a farm labourer, and he earned . . . with their big family . . . just enough money to buy bread. And that's all and my grandmother used to work on the tailoring . . . all day long.'

Miss Beech of Wormingford made the same point:

> 'My granny of course was a widow. When she started this there was no pension. They had to go on poor relief, they got a shilling a week and, of course, the quartern loaf, and of course you were a pauper.'

> *'Did the friends of your grandmother in Wormingford do the tailoring because their husbands' wages were not enough?'*

> 'Mmmm, their husband's wages were very low and of course there was nothing but parish relief . . . tailoring was the only thing that brought in anything else.'

In the town of Colchester itself, wages were low and wives of casual labourers or builders needed to supplement the husband's wage:

> *'Did your mother do the tailoring at all?'*

> 'Yes, my mother did tailoring, 'Cos she had to keep us going. Dad didn't earn very much. He was a master painter and decorator and you always had to wait for your money if you did anything like that, because he used to work . . . up Lexden way and they don't pay up like we do, you see, they didn't in those days anyway and Mum used to do coats at home from the factories. . . . She used to work very hard for the little she got . . . to make ends meet you see.'

Mrs Marsh's father was also a decorator and her mother took in tailoring:

> '*Do you think she did it for pin money or because she needed it?*'

> 'Oh no. Because she needed it. My father was in the house-decorating trade, of course all the winter they were out of work. They only could work when the weather was fine.'

Mrs Potter herself took in tailoring as her mother had done before her. She felt that her mother had been in more desperate need than herself and most of the informants felt this:

> '*Do you think your mother did the tailoring for a bit of pocket money?*'

> 'My mother did that bit of tailoring to feed us kids. She didn't do that for a bit of pocket money, she did that to keep us. She had 11 in 12 years, she had twins, she was having babies every year.'

> 'My husband didn't earn a lot when we got married. I used to have £2 a week housekeeping but with my 30 bob what I could earn helped didn't it? That helped me buy little extras for my children that I wouldn't've been able to have given if I hadn't worked, see? Yes, 'cos there was no allowance for children, if you had children, well that was your own fault, it was up to you to turn round and keep 'em which I done.'

The sorts of work women did were contingent on their family responsibilities. For unmarried women, their jobs were seen as, and often were, temporary. This meant that employers had little interest in training them for skilled and well-paid jobs. They themselves had little incentive to strive for higher wages in this situation. Domestic ideology had an enormous impact on the sort of jobs married women could do.

One of the few options open to them was to take in homework. Homeworking meant that they could look after their families, fulfil their domestic responsibilities and not contradict the prevailing ideology while also earning some money.

It seems clear that the notion that homeworkers worked for pin money is erroneous. Some of them may have had husbands whose wages were adequate to support the family. Most of them, however, were wives of agricultural workers, sailors and casual workers whose wages were low and seasonal. Many of them were widows with no other source of income. In both cases their earnings were vitally necessary.

Oral evidence makes the crucial link between the working life of tailoresses and their family life. The women who worked as tailoresses did not view their lives as separated between 'home and work'. This is particularly true of homeworkers who would often switch from paid work to unpaid work for the family while still sitting at the sewing machine.

Notes

1. Board of Trade, *Report of an Enquiry into the Earnings and Hours of the Labour of the Workpeople of the United Kingdom in 1906* 1909.
2. R. H. Tawney, *The Establishment of Minimum Rates in the Tailoring Industry under the Trade Boards Act of 1909* 1915, p. 129.
3. B. Hutchins, 'Statistics of Women's Life and Employment', *Journal of the Royal Society*, vol. 72, 30 June 1909, p. 218.
4. Clementina Black, *Married Women's Work* 1913, p. 74.

4 'What About That Lass of Yours Being in the Union?': Textile Workers and Their Union in Yorkshire, 1888–1922

JOANNA BORNAT

In attempting to describe and explain the development of a particular trade union – the General Union of Textile Workers – during the first twenty years of this century, the deficiencies of the conventional approach to trade union history became obvious. A union which has no past glories, no militant tradition, no craft splendours to portray, will perhaps feel less conscious of its own history, for whatever reason. Few minute books, the life blood of the trade union historian, survived for this union. One reason for this historical neglect may be the high proportion of women in the woollen and worsted industry within which the General Union grew. The production of woollen and worsted textiles has always involved women's labour at varying stages in different historical periods. Clapham, writing in 1907, estimated that in the West Riding of Yorkshire as a whole one in twelve men and boys and one in four women and girls were entering the industry.[1] Women, mainly in the 13–29 age group, were predominant in the manufacturing side of the industry. This means that any account which talks simply of 'the members', 'labour' or even of 'the weavers', would be guilty of inaccuracies in key areas unless the meaning of work and labour for men and women workers within a particular socio-economic context were also included.

The conventional approach has solid theoretical foundations in the notion of the separation of home and work. This concept has been used in a wide range of studies. It emphasises the effects of the physical separation of home and work as factory employment and capitalist ownership came to predominate. The concept stresses mobility, the development of a nuclear family structure and the throwing into competition of individuals who previously, it is argued, worked in some form of productive unity within the family. Following from this, the family is shown as having moved from the economic sector to the social sector as it becomes an instrument for consumption rather than of production. Latterly, the notion of the nuclear family as essential to the progress of industrialisation has been substantially modified, and the role of the family in the political economy of capitalism has come to be stressed. However, some aspects of this general theory still persist. As industrialisation develops a fixed pattern of relationships, the working woman in industry is depicted as liberated through the separation of home and work. This analysis is developed in most detail by Peter Stearns who sees the young woman factory workers at the turn of the century as mistress of her own due to her earnings. He draws a vivid contrast between the independence of the young working woman and her depressed and enslaved married sister.[2]

The conventional trade union approach and the stress placed on the physical separation of home and work are part of a tradition which draws attention away from the interrelationship of the work situation and the domestic economy. An analysis which sees home simply in terms of reproduction, socialisation and consumption neglects the surviving yet changed economic relationships which family members must play within the capitalist mode of production. To say that capitalism needs the family is not the simple story of the exploitation of its members. It is also the story of how those members learn to survive and support one another within the constraints of the wage labour–capital relationship.

I am arguing for an approach which seeks to understand men and women, their institutions, interactions and self-conceptions, in terms of their living and working relationships. The theoretical approach which seems most promising is that which attempts to articulate dimensions of class *and* dependency. By class I mean the relationship between wage labour and capital. By dependency I mean the unequal relationship between men and women main- tained through social and economic means.

In order to obtain a more complete understanding of these issues within a particular context of employment, I have interviewed women and men who entered the woollen manufacturing industry between the years of 1900 and 1916 in the Colne Valley of West

Yorkshire, a geographically compact area. Oral evidence provides an insight into the place of work in a community dominated by wool textile production. Thus, socialisation into patterns of work discipline, expectations about work, mobility within and between occupations in the industry, conflicts and solidarities within a mill can be reconstructed from the personal accounts of those who were to a large extent brought up in the industry.

Colne Valley has its unique characteristics in terms of products, ownership and typical form of mill organisation. Consequently, those brought up to work in its main industry were to differ in their experiences from those who, for example, grew up in Bradford, where other industries, such as engineering and building, together with a more elaborate structure of service and tertiary occupations, presented competing opportunities. In addition, the organisation of worsted production was dissimilar and in many ways presented a more highly segregated array of occupations. Nevertheless, the basic features of mill life and of textile production in this period are shared. Recruitment for an industry which required a mass of semi-skilled machine operators and minders with varied job security and low earnings, was bound to show particular characteristics.

There are three main points considered where the close interrelation of home and work are evident. These are, firstly, the transition from home to work, secondly, the destiny of the wage and thirdly, training in work. The final section will discuss trade union membership, how this was acquired, and how it operated.

In the transition from school to work, consideration of the home situation overrode other factors. This was true for both boys and girls in working class homes at this time. All left school at the earliest possible opportunity on attaining *Standard VII*, the top class, at their thirteenth birthday and most went straight to work at the mill:

'My idea was to get to be 13 as quickly as I could so that I could get in the mill and earn some money.'

'You don't think about it when you're a child you see. You know you've to get up and you were just shoved into the mill – that's all.'

'Oh they was waiting for you in them days. It wasn't bad getting a job in them days, not when I started work'

Some had left even earlier than 13 to do half time at 12 years of age, though this was becoming a decreasing practice, especially for girls, by 1914. One girl described her mother failing to get a full time place for her older half-time brother:

'And she went for his full-time papers to see about his full-time papers and they said, "oh well, they hadn't come." She said, "we'll have another half-timer." So she put me down for half-timer.'

Those who delayed their entry into mill work were in no sense idle at home. There were younger children to be cared for, domestic tasks, and occasionally work in a family shop. For one girl the First World War came as something of an opportunity:

'And when I went weaving the first it was at when the First World War started. I wasn't going to have to go weaving to see. [She was lame]. But I were glad when war started in me own mind and I knew I shouldn't have to stop at home. I used to think, I'm a little slavey enough without that.'

For one girl staying at home was a short-lived experience however:

'They was going to keep me at home with the business but I started sort of running about like they do when they're young and me mother said she thought I wanted some proper work and, you know, proper master like.'

What alternatives were presented to these young workers? To what extent was there any element of choice at the point of job entry? Apart from service and occasional shopwork there were no other alternatives. Several mentioned possibilities which they had not been allowed or had not wanted to take up:

'The teachers wanted you to stay on?'

Yes, the headmaster wanted me to – know if I could go to grammar school. But I just felt as if I had to go to work. We all had in those days . . . I didn't think I wanted to go. It wasn't me parents that stopped me. Probably they'd have let me go if I'd, if

I'd wanted you know. I suppose I should want to go working like me friends was. We all thought we had to go in the mill in those days you know.'

'And why did you not go into dressmaking?'

'Well, for the simple reason that you had to pay to learn and you'd no wages. You'd no wages. If you learned your trade you'd no wages. [The schoolmaster] came to see father and he wanted to compensate me father, moneywise, to let me go to a higher school and to train for a schoolmaster. And me father wouldn't. Well I could have gone to dressmake – but mother didn't seem to fancy us going then you see.'

Domestic service appears to become less popular by the later date and at any rate seems to have been rated extremely low as an occupation by local girls:

'Do you know the first time I went to Barnsley, her aunt says, "Do you still work in the mill?" I says "Yes". She says, "Oh you are common." I says, "Well I think skivvies are common." She says, "And what do you call skivvies?" I says, "Servants", I says, "we're not servants, we can please ourselves when we come and go. Skivvies can't." And I let her know what I thought about her. I says, "You mustn't think you're better than what we are because we consider that the girls in Barnsley, that have to go into service are very unlucky."'

Dressmaking might be a possibility for the younger delicate girl in a large family but it was out of the question when the family needed the young worker's wage. Even the four shillings brought in by the young girl above was a vital contribution.

The influence of locality, the pull of the home and parents seem to have been irresistible in forming choice. Mill work was considered the only job: 'We never thought of anything else.'

Children and young people came into the mills from differing backgrounds, not solely those found close to the mill gates themselves. The need for employment, an environment which was work-orientated and which was dominated by one industry, had a definite socialising effect which helped prepare the younger members of the valley townships for a working life and mill discipline.

Apart from the needs of the family economy there were social controls of a variety of types which helped shape attitudes to work. Elizabeth Roberts has shown how in Lancaster and Barrow, children's early exposure to the form and content of working life came through work, play and family life.[3] Carrying dinners, for perhaps sixpence a week, into the mills for workers at mid-day, might be done for pocket money, or the family budget, but this was also one way of becoming familiarised with not only the noise and characteristics of particular processes, but also the hierarchy of personnel within the mill:

'I used to go up during the school holidays and me mother used to sit me on the loom . . . I used to go up and take their dinner. You know Granny used to make them some dinner. And I used to come all up through Milnsbridge . . . I'd a good half hour's walk. Me Granny used to make them pies . . . and she used to put them in hot, straight out of the oven and wrap them in old towels and put them in a basket. And I had to trail all up there with them. And I used to go at dinner time and I'd stop while about three o'clock.'

There were, too, many aspects of this industry which surrounded the youngest members of the community. Living near the mills and with most families having at least one worker, the pattern of mill life dominated each day. Knockers-up might be paid to tap on windows or call out a name, but in most places it was the factory buzzers which called workers each morning and which marked their letting out at dinner time and at night. In small communities such as the Colne Valley townships, the mills dominated all aspects of life. Conversations at meal times, at home and between neighbours and friends would be filled with allusions to family members' work, changes in employment, brushes with bosses at work and comments on difficulties with materials and happenings at work. Such a mill-orientated climate left the younger people with fairly limited horizons, as respondents recalled:

'At home all the talk about work was about weaving. You don't think about it when you're a child you see. You know you've just to get up and you were shoved into the mill. That's all.'

'They never thought of it – I don't think it was ever thought of in our district it was always the mill, or you was a bit better off, getting into a shop or learning to dressmake or something like that you see.'

'It came from one generation to another. You see, your father was a weaver, you went weaving.'

The desire to become a worker and thus a contributor to the family income was overwhelming. Payment of the first wage could be a red-letter day:

'It was an exciting moment you know that, when you went home with your wages. I should be pleased I daresay, I was contributing.'

Real pride and feelings of elevated status were involved for a wage earner was a worker and families needed workers. However, despite the fact that so many had had first hand experience of the noise and dirt of mill life before they started earning, the first day's work could still come as a shock. A woman who began as a winder, as many young girls did, felt:

'It was a bit, shall I say, frustrating at first you know. You wondered what was happening. You see you were in the weaving shed and all the looms were clattering away you see. And all the noise till its a bit overpowering when you're so young.'

Another girl, just arriving from a mining village at 16, vividly recalled her first day as a doffer at the Globe worsted:

'Oh I kept going to boss, "What time is it?" "So and so." Oh I thought it were a damned long day. Good God. And I'd see him again, "What time is it?" "Art tha lost lass?" I says, "I must be". Anyway, when I got home me mother says, "How have you got on?" "Don't ask me. My God, Don't ask me," I says. "I've asked about time about fifty times," I says. "That fellow will be thinking me a damn nut." So I got me tea, half on it, fell asleep, got in rocking chair. Mother, "Hey, come on lass, it's bedtime, twelve o'clock," "Ooh," I says, "My God is it?" . . . a woman telled to me mother it were oil at made you sleep, smell o'toil and that . . . Oh my God.'

The industry needed young workers. Finding work was no problem. In some cases mills actively sought families, especially those with large numbers of girls:

'*Why did you move to Slaithwaite?*'

'Well there was a man came from Slaithwaite to see, with there being such a lot of girls you know. They used to seek families up that had a lot of girls, to go and work in the mills . . . if they heard tell of anybody that had a family of girls they used to go and seek them up and get them to go work in the mill.'

The industry certainly exerted a real pull, but, work, home and family remained closely linked. This is clearly seen in the actual finding of a job, the final stage in the transition from school to work. If the freedom conferred by wage labour status and the needs of industry were really paramount, then the influence of home would appear minimal. However, this was not the case.

'*And how did you get your job?*'

'Oh they was waiting for you. It wasn't bad getting a job in them days, not when I started work. You see me sister worked there for a start. When she started – she were first – me mother knew the foreman when she were going to see. So she went to his house. And he told her to come morning after you see, and start. Well with her being there you see, she arranged for me to go.'

Even those who went independently to seek work had experienced socialisation into the customs and practices. Taking sisters, relatives or neighbours their dinners, or listening to conversations in houses close to mills where friends and relatives might gather to eat their food, could provide information and introductions to opportunities. In one case a girl had only to cross the street in which she lived to ask for a job. Most were helped across this first bridge by mothers, fathers, sisters and aunts:

'I was ill away from school. And I went to me Auntie. They used to take dinners to the workers you see. *A* d I went with me Auntie to take her son's dinner and she asked for me because it was coming time for me to start at bobbin winding.'

The usual first job was bobbin winding, for girls, at a wage of five shillings a week, But relatives already in some skilled employment could secure entry to preferred jobs:

'My sister was what they call a mender. And of course it was supposed to be both a skilled job and a job they could earn middlin' a money. And not as dirty as some of the other jobs. So when I was going to the mills she asked if I could go and learn to mend straightaway.

*   *   *

  I went with me mother . . . me mother had always worked at Hoyle's. And like she said, she wanted me under her eye you see. And I got with a young lady warping and there was two warpers that were needing – we were called clerkers.'

The second point at which family and work can be seen to interact is the disposition of the wage. Historian Peter Stearns says that in England daughters paid board and room to their parents; on the Continent they turned their wages over directly.[4] This assumption seems to be based on the evidence from the Report published by the Board of Trade in 1911 of the *Survey of Accounts of Expenditure of Wage Earning Women and Girls*. However, even among the 30 case studies published by the Board of Trade there are six women who give their wages intact to their mothers. Other interviews present no constant pattern of paying board for this country. There are both regional and social differences. I want to argue that the difference between paying board and 'tipping up' (turning over) a wage to the family, represented by the mother, was crucial in both the relationship of the wage earner to the family and the wider economic significance of the wage beyond the point of production.
  Although economic independence may appear as a natural corollary of waged employment, the theoretical freedom of the wage earner was actually limited in a number of ways. The interdependency of wage earner and family was based upon issues

of survival. Thus the family in capitalist society is not only a creation of economic relationships but also a response to these, a necessary adaptation and expression of the will to survive. Tipping up a wage to the family related directly to the needs of the family unit and its individual members. This means that gender, age, and economic circumstances all helped determine the incidence of tipping up.

Wages were usually tipped straightaway and intact to the mother. Only two mentioned giving their wages to anyone else. These were girls who for various reasons lived in their grandparent's home. Their grandmothers received the wage:

'It was 12s 6d. And I said to me mother, can I give it me granny? She said, yes, you can. And I gave my first week's wage to me granny, because she'd always been so good to me.'

Local and general custom decreed that a 'penny in the shilling' could be kept for pocket money: 'Mother got the wage and I got 5 pence.'

As wages rose gradually from the normal starting point of 5 shillings for a girl, slightly more for a boy, to somewhere about the pound level before the First World War, more could be kept for spending on amusements, entertainment, or for saving towards holidays or marriage. However, the family's needs still came first:

'I went home and others were buying a cream slice with the twopence of the wage. We'd so much and this bonus on because of the war. And we'd this out of the wage and I know I bought this cream slice. I didn't half get it for it.'

The amount kept back is less significant than the actual tipping of the wage. What was left for spending or saving was determined not by the wage earner but by the parents and by the relationship of the individual earner to the parents plus family. This could affect girls more adversely than boys:

'Our Herbert were married and there was only me and me brother next to me. And then he were paying board and I had to tip all me wages up.'

'Why did he pay board while you tipped your wages up?'

'Oh well, that's a question, isn't it? . . . I know me mother gave me some spends and I daren't spend it because I was frightened we might want a meal during the week. And I said, Well you'll have to give me mother more money. I says, can't see why you should be going out every night a week and if me mother doesn't give me half a dollar – I can't go out. Put some more money in.'

Accounts of tipping up are graphic and resentment was experienced repeatedly as one man recalled:

'And I said one Friday night, I were coming up to being married. It'd be about 12 month before I got married. And one Friday night – me mother used to sit there with her apron open and we used to tip all our wages into her apron, me father, me and me sister. And I said to me Father, I thought, Oh I'll try it on, and I just – and he's got a big moustache, he'd a Jimmy Edwards moustache had me father you know. And I says, Oh father, I'm thinking of starting paying board. You see I were earning about six or seven quid a week then, spinning, which was a good wage then. And I just looked at his moustache. When – it used to drop some way when he were disappointed or angry. And he looked straight back at me and the only words he said to me were, If you do, you'll be the first one that ever has done at this house. And I says, right. And I tipped every penny up to me mother up to getting – before I was getting married.'

The feeling that as the young worker grew older he or she might be the local exception to the tipping up custom was frequently expressed. This may have been due to the fact that the determinants of tipping up were specific to each family in the sense that each family differed as to parents' occupations, numbers of siblings, ratios between sexes and age of parents. In general, however, it seems that tipping up continued until the son or daughter left to form their family or formed their own home in the parents' home. Those who never left or who married later than most, in their thirties and forties, only stopped tipping up their mothers died or became too infirm to manage household affairs:

'I gave me mother . . . my wages until I was well over 20. And she said, well, and she had got to that state that she couldn't do either shopping or housekeeping or anything – and she said, what's the good of giving it me – it's you that have it to see to.'

An alternative to tipping up could be provided by going into lodgings for a boy. Those who talk of paying board at an earlier stage than leaving the parental home were saving towards an announced marriage and might be fortunately placed in the family, for example, a younger sister to older brothers. Family composition could be crucial:

> 'We could have new clothes you see and me mother used to make all our dresses . . . when she'd got those workers we had, we could have the best of hats . . . the best of coats. I remember having two pairs of shoes at once. One was ordinary shoes . . . and then we had some rinking boots . . . and oh, we thought we were well off then. Well we were. But you see it did away with all, anything like that when the First World War started because we'd no workers.' (Her five older brothers went as soldiers.)

Those who did pay board, and they seem to have been few, were those whose family circumstances were comfortably secure, whose fathers were shopkeepers, skilled textile craftsmen or foremen.

The question of the mother's role as receiver of this wage suggests the possibility of economic power for the woman, within the domestic situation. It also links the domestic economy with the cash nexus at the point of production. In law, the woman was dependent, politically she scarcely existed, and yet she had the key role in maintaining and servicing the family members. Her banker's role was determined however by her husband's legal powers, his wllingness to tip up his wages and the wages of the other dependents in the family.

The third area of relations between work and family is that of training at work. Unlike cotton and outside the craft and supervisory jobs which are almost exclusively male, there were no examples of controlling entry from the mill floor, nor was the system of subcontracting as general. Those girls and women who learned warping and weaving would not be paid during the few weeks of learning. It was only after the First World War that mills themselves began to pay weavers as they taught, a final recognition that monetary loss to the weaver had been involved as well as gains to the concern:

'And you see they do lose something with learning. Because you
see, unless they tell you what to do and stop your loom and tell
you what's this and that you throw them out a lot. In fact you used
. . . to learn a fortnight and if somebody was learning you used to
have to pay them to learn. You used to have to give them
something to learn you to weave.'

There was thus a convention that learners would pay their teachers,
but there were ways of circumventing this.

First jobs for 13-year-olds entering the mill were usually winding
for girls and reaching-in for boys in weaving sheds – doffing for
either sex in spinning. These jobs would be taught by fellow workers
and would be learned within a day or two at the most. The more
skilled jobs of warping, weaving and mending required lengthier
training of perhaps two weeks in the case of weaving and even
longer in the case of warping and mending.

The one occupational group amongst women workers which was
accorded high standing was the menders: 'They were the aristocrats
of the mill then – menders'; 'the warpers could earn a lot more
money than us and then the menders could earn more than the
warpers'; 'they always used to think that menders were kind of
better . . . it seems as though they were a bit higher in the social
scale.' Such perceptions were based on the realities of higher
earnings, better working conditions and a position of some responsibility for the finished or almost finished piece of cloth. Moreover,
mending jobs, in proportion to other jobs in mills were fewer and
open only to workers with experience in the mill or with family
connections in the mending room. If workers perceived these
distinctions it was because of the very real advantages which
mending presented as an occupation. For a woman, mending could
present the ideal job:

'It's the best paid job in the West Riding is mending. They even
have it in their homes . . . Some that have a spare bedroom would
have it up in the bedroom you see, and they could just go and do a
bit when they wanted.'

'They were menders for life . . . you see they used to have
mending at home. Oh yes, they used to have the pieces brought
in.'

The practice of fining also had its distancing effect in terms of relating mending to other occupations in the mill. Money taken as fines from weavers' wages, was, in some mills, paid to menders as a bonus.

There were many tasks to learn and the more complicated weaving machinery took some managing. The most usual way of by-passing the question of cash payment to a worker-teacher was of course to contain the function within the family or wider kin network. If there was no weaver, worker or mender in the immediate family then family friends could take on the job and again direct cash loss could be avoided:

'I know they used to pay a pound a week perhaps to learn to weave. But it was a friend of me mothers that learned me and she wouldn't take anything.'

The young worker's career through the mill was punctuated by frequent job changes sometimes in pursuit of more wages, other times in search of experience. More congenial working conditions and the location of a skilled uncle or father who would teach a weaver might also influence mobility. The girl who stayed put was a rarity and few made only one more. Mills varied in size from perhaps only a score of looms to several hundreds. This meant that to get a loom a would-be weaver might have to leave her twisting place to find not only training but a guarantee of a machine. Under such conditions of mobility and uncertainty, family ties could be a positive advantage for quite a number of years.

Such ties could have their disadvantages too. Rules of precedence in the family would determine choice of action in times when work was short, as happened to one young woman:

'Now then, I was one of the last to finish really but I had an uncle that was a weaver up there as well and when it came to my turn I let him have it because he had a wife and child – we had the business going on so I let me uncle . . . have my place.'

More immediately, of course, those working with relatives endured a closer supervision than other workers:

'Me dad worked there and he asked for me. He wanted me to get
there . . . and it were a pity he ever did. Because you know if ever
I did owt they always told me dad. He always knew. He used to
say we were too long at toilets you know.'

Another girl had her brother-in-law for her overlooker:

'I didn't like me brother-in-law . . . I think he made me work
harder than anyone else. So they wouldn't think he was . . .
giving me a favour.'

She went to complain about something at the office:

'Well if there was anything we wanted altering, a few of us would
go into the office and of course I was the one. And the man that
owned he'd say, And you ——, he'd say, —— your brother-in-
law. I'd say, well what difference does it make? I says, The
wrong's there just whether ——'s my overlooker or not. You
know, I stuck up for myself.'

Perhaps it was easier to be forward with a relative in a supervisory
position, but presumably he would make sure that challenges to
authority were made in a containable way.

It is only by following in such detail the family involvement in the
work process and in particular the different experience and
expectations of boys and girls, men and women that the role of
women in trade unions can be understood.

*   *   *

In order to break with official accounts and conventional explanations of women's trade-union behaviour, we need not only to
appreciate the nature of unions but also to see them within a given
context of social and economic relationships. Trade unions are a
product of capitalist society and must therefore play a part in
reflecting and reproducing the social and economic relationships
which persist in the dominant institutions in that society. In so far as
they seek only to control conditions at the point of production, and
take no wider social or economic focus, they will necessarily take a
narrow view of the function of the wage in capitalist society. Trade

union historians following this narrow focus derived from the consequent range of trade union documents, and from an acceptance of this narrow definition of the scope of trade unionism, provide us with explanations of women's membership which are inaccurate and often insufficient.

Women are regarded both by trade-union officials and their historians as either a menace to be kept at bay or as allies with limited fighting potential. Fox, in his history of the boot and shoe industry's unions takes the typical approach when he suggests that the fortunes of women trade unionists in this industry were determined by the politics and personalities of two particular women between 1910 and 1940.[5] These women, it is argued, have definite effects on the union at two different points in its history both before and after the war, effects which are short-term and appear to fade as their originators either drop out of activity or retire from the union. this analysis avoids an examination of basic social and economic relationships and places women's involvement in a 'problem' centred framework. It does not explain the persistence through varied phases in a union's history of certain patterns of involvement, not only for women but perhaps for the wider membership of both men and women.

An alternative approach is one which sees unions as men's institutions and women's involvement as determined and limited by a domination based on sexual inequality.[5] However, this on its own is not a sufficient explanation. We need to know about the conditions for both the emergence and the perpetuation of such dominance and the ways in which trade union policies and structures reflected and expressed the relationships particularly in the notion of women's dependency.

Dependency in the work situation is maintained through the assumption of women's work as marginal. That is, marginal not only in terms of a woman's life as such, but marginal to the whole area of work as conceived in terms of men's labour and its rewards. In real terms marginality is confirmed through exclusion from skilled occupations; the payment of a smaller amount in wages; defined areas of employment – service, subsidiary and casual. Literary and spoken confirmation of these conditions is passed on through education and the words of observers, theorists and commentators who, even today, still persist in describing the English working class as if it comprised only male, often only independent celibates. The effect of the conferring of marginal status on women was realised in the 'dilution' crises of the First World War when men's skilled jobs in engineering were sub-divided into semi-skilled tasks for women. These were in fact totally predictable, only dramatised by the forcing conditions of a wartime economy.

There are particular features in the structure, organisation and ideology of trade unions which can be seen as expressions of the dominant factor, marginality. Barbara Drake in her study shows the exclusively male origins of all major unions at the turn of the century and shows that even in the cotton unions, thought generally to have had an advanced policy with regards to women members, much was left to be desired.[6] She refers to unions which charged a lower level of subscription and therefore paid less in benefits to women members. The custom of excluding low-scale contributors from office had not long passed. The double work load of most working women is of course an enduring feature. The Webbs in discussing organisation amongst cotton weavers, refer to the disadvantage of needing a large staff of paid collectors to secure the regular payment of contributions from the girls and married women who were unwilling to bring their weekly pence to the public house in which the branch meeting was still frequently held.[7]

The establishment of Socialist Clubs and Trade Union premises went some way in subsequent years towards neutralising the problems associated with collection in public houses in open situations. However, the predominantly male clientele of the Clubs as reflected in the nightly attractions offered, beer and billiards, did not go very far in improving the situation as far as young working women were concerned.

Two areas in particular highlight the particular relationship of women to the union as structured by their marginality to the world of work. These are the role of men in persuading women members of their families to join unions and the system of house-to-house collection of union dues. In discussion, and without prompting women tended to mention their father or uncle's influence in the question of joining:

> 'When we went to —— and ——'s, everybody had to be in. there were people in the union . . . me father learned me and as soon as ever I got onto a loom of me own, man went: What about that lass of yours being in the union?'

Her account is revealing because she shows the appeal being made over her head rather than directly to her. Another woman was recruited by her uncle and describes what happened in appropriate Yorkshire speech:

'I asked me uncle —— if he'd learn me to weave at ——'s. And he said, yes. So I went and he says, I'll tell thee summat, he just talked like that . . . he says, Tha's to join the union before tha starts. I says, How do you mean? He says, I'll tell thee that's to join union afore tha starts weyving.'

One girl who never joined explained why:

'Me father wasn't a member of the union and so we weren't encouraged to join a union.'

This is not to say that weavers taught by women friends or relatives did not also join the union when they got their looms, they did of course in those mills where unions were accepted. These were few enough before the First World War. However, the role of male relatives in presenting union membership is significant. Young workers would be about 16 or 18 when they first acquired a loom suggesting that union membership was seen as an accompaniment of increased age and skill. The exclusion of the young and less skilled either by neglect or design was always to be a weakness in textile union activities.

The recruitment of women to the union was often posed in family, paternal terms. The unions' press, the *Yorkshire Factory Times* contains frequent appeals to male members to ensure that the women in their families became union members. In February 1915 the anonymous columnist 'Sweeper-up'[8] castigates Bradford's men trade unionists:

'These 24 000 Trade Unionists are in close relationship to 15 000 women textile workers, but very few of them help the women in Trade Union matters or with Trade Union advice, and I cannot withdraw my observations that many of them are half Trade Unionists and semi-blacklegs as a consequence.'

In the paper the following week Ben Turner is recorded as expressing the same opinions at an ILP meeting in Bradford. His

New Year Resolutions for the union in 1916 include the vow that everyone in 'his house should be a Trade Union member, especially the women.'[9]

In 1915, a joint conference of GUTW representatives and Bradford Trades Council Executive held to consider the question of improved organisation of Bradford Women resolved amongst other things to send each male Trade Union member a circular suggesting he encourage the women members of his family to join the union. Although accurate figures are hard to come by it would appear that roughly half the union's members at any one time were women. Clapham writing in 1907 put the membership at 1500 of whom 631 were women. Turner's history of the union mentions 110 000 paying members, the bulk of whom were women and young persons, but about 30 per cent were men.[10] Despite these proportions, participation by women in the management and control of the union was minimal.

The war brought some changes. In 1920 Keighley District had a woman secretary with a committee of 11 women and one man. Bradford showed a proportion of 10 men to 8 women in its District Committee. However at the highest level in the union men still predominated. There were 21 men and only 6 women on the executive committee in 1920. For a short period during the war the union had had a woman organiser and a Women's Guild which had had no power to do anything but deliberate and advise. This is not to say that some women, particularly in the Bradford area, were not active and vociferous members of the union. The point is that the framework of union government and power was dominated by men and the language of agitation was for the main part couched in terms relative to men workers. It was to this institution that young working women were expected to look for representation on wages and work matters.

The women interviewed in Colne Valley had few positive statements to make about trade union membership. None had ever considered approaching the union over a shopfloor matter such as bad work or unjust treatment from a superior. Their association with the union was largely indirect. For this group of workers payment of the weekly subscriptions was usually carried out at the doorstep by mothers and grandmothers from the family kitty on behalf of the young worker to a collector who worked on a house-to-house basis.

'*And did you pay your subscription from your wage – or how was it paid?*'

'It was out of me wages yes.'

'*And you paid it yourself did you?*'

'No they used to come to the house for the union.'

'*Would your mother give it to them?*'

'Yes.'

Just used to come – no they wouldn't let them collect it in the mill. They didn't like the unions you see in the mill . . . None of them. They didn't want you to be in a union. They could pay what they wanted if you wasn't in the union. If you was in the union they didn't like it.'

'*So they came round the house for the money?*'

'Yes, yes, more or less.'

'*And would your mother give your money, or did you give the money?*'

'Oh well – it came out of the wage.'

'Me dad made me be in . . . He was a strong union man.'

'*How did you pay your dues to the union?*'

'Well there was a collector used to come for them . . . he used to come about once a month. And it wasn't so much at that time. You used to have to pay him.'

'*And did you pay or did your father pay for you?*'

'Well I had – well it'd be paid with all the lot I expect. We were all in.'

Even one woman who worked in a well organised mill where collections took place on the mill floor recalled that her father, who also worked there, paid her subscriptions for her. Those who paid board might have paid their own subscriptions of course. At its moment of highest activity union membership under these conditions was only a defence, but most commonly it took its place with other contemporary forms of social insurance.

The combined effects of economic marginality and dependent status helped sustain unequal rates of pay in the industry. In Colne Valley, women and men weavers wove side by side on the same work. However, the facts of life at work were such that women received roughly 10 per cent less in wages. Men were paid more, it was argued, because they could lift the finished pieces from the looms and made fewer demands on the turners. These were debatable points which at any rate were not really central to the question of production. As one woman clearly saw it:

> 'Oh I don't think it's right that a man have to have more money. We've said so many a time, because they didn't do anything any different.'

> 'They carried pieces and stuff.'

> 'Well they only lifted them off, they never carried them. They'd only to lift them into a cart. That's all. And the turner took them away . . . Lifted the empty beams out and that's all they did. And lifted the piece off.'

*　　*　　*

I have tried to develop certain themes, both theoretical and methodological, concerning men and women's work experience, particularly as it affected their relationship to a trade union. The great reward from oral history is the confirmation of historical research and the suggestion of new insights into previously researched areas. In the case of the Colne Valley textile workers, the interview material suggests that Trade Union history may be understood not only in terms of the expression of its most advanced sections but also in terms of those less well documented officially.

Again, an analysis solely in terms of trade union based conflict in the factory ignores the significance of paid work to different members of a family at different points in that family's life cycle. Housework and childcare can be seen as closely related to paid work when we followed the course of the wage as it enters the household beyond its being earned and paid out in the workplace. The early twentieth-century family is thus seen not only as a product of capitalist relations of production with its formally independent wage earners, its physical separation from the place of work and the forced contribution of all its members to the wage earning process whether in paid work or not. It can also function as a means of survival, a dual role. Although binding its women members especially close, the family can also provide the means to by-pass some of the purely competitive aspects of the labour market. On the other hand, the pooling of the wage, in theory providing a form of security to individuals at the mercy of the system of production, has to be set against its effect on women and young persons whose lesser wages may be more subject to the varying economic fortunes of the family unit. This is especially the case, I would suggest, for women, since the assumed marginality of their involvement in the sphere of paid work weakens their attachment and claim to the wage. Being kept at home as a child or young helper at home or as an adult housewife is indicative of low productive status in the economy where wage earning is, of necessity, rated highly.

All such factors should interest the trade union historian and help to lead us away from such simplistic formulations as woman's apathy and disinclination for collective action, which in the main have been seen as explanations for union weakness or lack of growth.[11] The meaning of trade unionism in any historical context can be understood at two related levels. One concerns protection and defence against employer action. The other highlights the unions' part socially, not only in the sense of providing security, but also in providing explanations and perpetuating social relations between members of the working class.

Notes

1. J. H. Clapham, *The Woollen and Worsted Industries*, 1907, pp. 176–7.
2. Peter Stearns, 'Working-Class Women in Britain 1890–1914' in Martha Vicinus (ed.), *Suffer and Be Still*, 1972; Peter Stearns, *Lives of Labour*, 1975.
3. Elizabeth Roberts, 'Learning and Living – Socialisation outside school' in *Oral History*, vol. 3, no. 2.
4. Peter Stearns, 1975.

5. Alan Fox, *A History of the National Union of Boot and Shoe Operatives 1874–1957*, 1958.
6. Barbara Drake, *Women in Trade Unions*, 1921.
7. Sidney and Beatrice Webb, *Industrial Democracy*, 1898, especially the chapter: 'The Method of Collective Bargaining'.
8. 'Sweeper-Up' was the Union's president Ben Turner. In this column and undercover of anonymity he frequently passed comment on the union's affairs.
9. *Yorkshire Factory Times*, 6 January 1916.
10. H. A. Turner, *Trade Union Growth, Structure and Policy*, 1962.
11. Kate Purcell, 'Militancy and Acquiescence Amongst Women Workers', in S. Burman (ed.), *Fit Work for Women*, 1979.

5 'Educating Teacher': Women and Elementary Teaching in London, 1900–1914

FRANCES WIDDOWSON

The nineteenth century as a whole witnessed a rise in the status of the elementary teacher, but the period after 1870 saw a rapid acceleration in this process and a broadening of the social class base from which elementary school teachers were recruited. After the 1870 Education Act and subsequent Acts, which made elementary education both compulsory and free, the demand for elementary teachers rose rapidly. It was mainly working-class children who attended elementary schools since middle and upper-class children were educated at private schools or at home.

During the 1870s and 1880s lower middle-class girls entered elementary teaching in larger numbers and forming a growing proportion of the profession by the 1900s. Previous to this period, elementary schools had relied to a great extent on working-class recruits, and it is easy to see why. Middle-class men were not likely to be attracted by the low wages of the elementary teacher and middle-class women were restricted to certain genteel occupations if they were forced to earn their living, for example being a governess in a private school or in someone's home or being a lady's companion. Although the salary of the trained elementary school mistress was perhaps as attractive as that of a governess, there were definite reasons why this work was considered unsuitable. First, in the mid-nineteenth century, the training of the elementary teacher began early, at 12 or 13 years of age, and the pupil teacher was subject to a very hard and strenuous routine, teaching classes in the day and studying every evening. There were great fears that girls would become anaemic and ill because of the strain involved.[1] Thus girls from well-to-do homes were not likely to be put through this type of training. However it was possible to take the pupil teacher exams without undertaking the five year apprenticeship as a pupil teacher. But unless special coaching was provided a girl from a private school was unlikely to pass these exams and qualify for a place at college.[2] Middle-class girls were often notoriously deficient in the 3 R's although well educated in other matters.

There were in any case, some unattractive features about training college life which continued to exist up to the 1870' and 80s. These colleges had a traditionally spartan routine dating back to their inception in the 1830s and 40s. This was intended to mould working class recruits into humble, hardworking teachers who could then return to schools able to instill Christian virtues into working children. By the 1870s, however, there was an increasing interest in opening up new work areas for middle-class girls and Louisa Hubbard and other feminists wrote pamphlets and letters to the press urging the daughters of clergymen, doctors and professional men to train and become elementary teachers.[3] There is little evidence that the more established middle-class groups took much notice, but among small professional men (architects, surveyors, minor civil servants, accountants and clerks) and their daughters there are signs that they heeded this advice was heeded and acted upon it.

Beside the effect of such feminist propaganda, there were significant changes in elementary schools by the end of the nineteenth century which helped to attract lower-middle-class girls. There was a gradual improvement in conditions – smaller classes, better buildings and sanitation and healthier children. In addition, new Day Colleges were opened in the 1890s which encouraged middle-class parents to allow their daughters to train while living at home. The National Union of Teachers had, by 1900, improved the status of the elementary teacher by establishing a pension scheme and minimum wage rates and increased security of tenure. These changes can be traced by using written sources such as College Records, Parliamentary Reports and educational periodicals, but it is important to get a clearer picture of how individual choices were made by girls who became elementary teachers.

There has been one major book written on the rising social status of the elementary school teacher in the nineteenth and twentieth centuries: A. Tropp's *The School Teachers*. This relies solely on written source material – educational periodicals, government publications and official union records. Although Tropp analyses the rise of the school teacher from a professional point of view he rarely describes the actual experience of being an elementary schoolmaster or mistress. Since it is growth of trade union consciousness that interests him, women teachers are relegated to the background. Most of his references are to teaching magazines for men rather than women, and the records of the National Union of Teachers up to the 1900s do not give one a sense of women teachers position and attitudes, because women teachers on the whole were not active participants on the National Executive. The few really active women members had grown dissatisfied with the NUT which refused to support equal pay for women teachers and they had left the NUT in 1909 to form their own National Union of Women Teachers. Even though women began to outnumber men as elementary teachers after 1870, Tropp mainly concentrates on the social status of the male teacher. At times he is guilty of judging the profession as a whole (men and women) by a predominantly male standard of social success. Thus for instance he postpones the date of the final stage of the elementary teachers entry into professional status until the interwar period when growing numbers of teachers were becoming candidates for municipal and parliamentary office. But surely such candidates were mostly men teachers and the achievement of these offices was primarily a sign of male success.

Other indices should be used to a assess the status of the woman elementary teacher. One can, indeed, claim that the status of the woman elementary teacher had risen more quickly than that of male elementary teachers. It is significant that recent American sociological studies have shown that women elementary teachers usually came from more advantaged homes than men. The reason given is that middle-class men have a greater range of jobs open to them while women have far fewer. In the period 1870–1925 this same pattern existed in Britain. There were even fewer careers open to educated women at that time and thus there was likely to be a greater disparity between the sexes as regards the way each viewed their jobs and social position. By going beyond the written sources and interviewing women teachers, the *women teacher*'s point of view can be kept in focus, her self-image and her view of elementary school mistresses as a whole. There are, of course, existing written source materials which are crucial to studying the social background of girls who were training to be elementary teachers. But even these can be usefully supplemented by using oral history techniques.

By examining Training College Records it is possible to find out about the social origins of students as I have done for Whiteland's Training College which was one of the new 20 residential training colleges opened between 1839 and 1840. Whitlelands, based in Chelsea, took only girls and its records give fathers' occupation for their students from 1847 to 1900. They show an increasing proportion of students coming from small professional or lower-middle class homes. Reports of the Cross Commission, 1886, and the Pupil Teacher Commission, 1898, contain information about the social origins of pupil teachers as it was regarded as desirable to widen the social base of recruits. The evidence presented in these Reports takes the form of interviews and is akin to oral history in that the witnesses give valuable personal impressions of the social origins of pupil teachers although they do not supply accurate quantitative evidence.

However there were some questions which even these written sources could not always answer. For instance, college records were often silent about mothers' occupation. Only in the case of students with widowed mothers alive was maternal occupation stated. Also college records gave no information about the position of the student in her family (i.e. youngest/eldest) and no information about the occupations of brothers and sisters, factors which might be crucial in influencing girls to become elementary teachers. All these areas can be covered by oral history, for example a family tradition of teaching can be uncovered by interviewing.

Statistics on public education can tell us that a certain percentage of pupil-teachers were the daughters of a particular social group but we also need to know why these particular girls were attracted to teaching and why other girls from the same social group turned to other jobs. The interviews were intended to bring to light the sort of image elementary school teaching had for girls in the 1900–25 period, for I hoped that in-depth interviews with women who had enetered this occupation would give me an entrée into the world of some elementary and secondary schoolgirls of the period. This would help evaluate the work opportunities which lay open to them, through *their* eyes rather than the eyes of those who were compiling career books at that time. How far did girls feel they had freely chosen their careers? Did they think they had actively wanted to teach in elementary schools or had they been pushed into by force of circumstances? How did they view their training college life? Had they known what to expect? Did they see it as a chance to be liberated from home life and instead enter a new world of books, debates and intellectual activity? Did they feel influenced by ideas that girls should be economically independent?

In order to assess why some girls took up elementary teaching and what their alternatives were in the 1900–25 period it was necessary to find our about their family backgrounds: social class, income and education. By asking about sisters' occupations I could also discover what clusters of jobs were considered suitable by these families for their daughters. Most of the respondents had some family connections with teaching but none had parents or grandparents who had been elementary school teachers themselves. But, significantly, quite a few had female cousins and sisters who had entered elementary teaching. Rarely did I find evidence of brothers entering this occupation. While a number of fathers had received some secondary education, very few mothers had had this opportunity. Many of the women I interviewed remembered how their mothers deeply regretted their own lack of education and their strong conviction that their daughters should have access to a secondary type of education. For their daughters, this meant passing an exam to get into the pupil teacher centre or gaining a county scholarship to a secondary school. For one or two it involved taking a special preliminary scholarship exam which later bound them to carry on training as elementary teachers.

In the 1900 to 1925 period, the wages of a skilled workman were roughly the minimum which would allow a family to send a daughter to training college. Of course the level of income could vary according to the number and ages of children within the family, but the expense of supporting a daughter first as a pupil teacher and then as a college student was such that it was usually beyond the means of father who were unskilled labourers.[4] The interviews made it clear that in most cases the strain on the family budget was continuous until the girl left college at 20. As pupil teachers and students in training, they did earn small amounts but this was more or less used up in buying books and equipment needed for studying and real wages did not start until they were fully qualified.

Mrs Thomas described how as a scholarship girl at secondary school and later when she got into the pupil teacher centre, she was given grants of money. She remembered her father borrowing from her, pleased to have this extra fund but she had to have the money back to buy the books she needed.

> 'I was sent a Post Office book with enough money to buy the books . . . I knew my father wanted to borrow the money so I went and got it . . . he said I could do with a bit of that money now and go and get it. I got it out and gave it him, but he had to give it back again because I had to pay for books, but he was glad of me getting a Post Office book.'

Most respondents from working-class homes emphasised that they felt rather abnormal being dependent on their families long after their elementary school friends had started earning their living. A few certainly envied these girls their increased economic independence and the gayer social life that it brought. Mrs Dublin, born in New Cross 1888, described her feelings when she attended the pupil teacher Centre at Deptford in SE London (1903–7):

> *'Did you envy the girls who went to work immediately in offices?'*

> 'I think I did rather. I used to think how lovely it would be to go to the city – till I was quite old I thought that . . . I had to trundle down to Deptford and I walked, it wasn't very bright and not very exciting you see. Girls who went to the city they had offices with men and women. And I, only a girl of course, I can't remember how many girls were in my class at the centre but *two* boys – but there was nothing very exciting about it – we used to have a social once a year there, that was quite nice, but nothing else, no outings – nothing . . . just work and very drab classrooms.
>   College was very different. I enjoyed college . . . it was very lively – very nice altogether – beautiful buildings and lovely grounds.'

The immense amount of moral support and encouragement girls received from their families, their mothers in particular, helped make both pupil teachers at centres and those at secondary school feel less frustrated about earning no money and having less independence than friends who were working. It was difficult to draw the line between lower middle class and respectable working class homes but it is particularly interesting to look at the situations of those whose fathers were in the clerk/small businessman category: in my interviews, these included Miss Marsden, born 1890, daughter of two ex-private school teachers whose father later became a clerk, Mrs Scott, born 1895 whose father owned a big tailoring business in Piccadilly, and Mrs Barker, born 1896 whose father was an ex naval instructor who took on the family clay pipe factory.

One point which came across in the interviews with these three respondents was the way elementary teaching was seen as the next best thing to going to university and becoming secondary school teachers, a possibility which never entered the range of jobs considered by more working class respondents. Miss Marsden and Mrs Scott emphasised how they had always wanted to teach since they were small children. Both had been to private schools till they were about 10 years old and Miss Marsden had had several governesses up to the age of 7 or 8. But at 10 they were transferred by their parents to Higher Grade schools in order to prepare for a Secondary School scholarship.

Although they admired their high school teachers greatly, they felt that the cost of getting a degree was prohibitive and they chose to become teachers at the elementary level. The idea of elementary teaching did not disturb them too much because they had previously attended a type of elementary school (Higher Grade). In retrospect Mrs Scott felt that her Higher Grade school had given her a false sense of security about elementary teaching for she was to find some ordinary elementary schools much less congenial. In both cases we can see the subsidised training offered by training colleges helping to attract those lower middle-class girls who had a very strong vocation to teach but limited financial resources. Their attendance at Higher Grade Schools was an important factor which helped ease them towards teaching in ordinary elementary schools. Miss Marsden was very aware of the fact that she came from a different social class to the average student at Goldsmiths College in 1910. She found the men students 'a brash lot':

'You know what a lot of these men were? They were very uneducated – uncivilized – put it that way. You used to find it with the teachers – when I was evacuated these teachers didn't know lots of things you'd expect everyone to know . . . a teacher who

worked at the hospital (doing Red Cross work) she didn't know
how to lay a table.'

'Did you find the men a bit rough?'

'Yes they fancied their luck. But they were in a different class of
society. I wouldn't mix with them out of college – not that lot! Oh
no way. I met one of the girls I was with after . . . she'd married
one of the men . . . one of our year at college.'

'You wouldn't have considered marrying one of them?'

'Oh not me.'

Mrs Barker decided that she wanted to teach because of the
example of her own elementary teachers. She described how she
was impressed at an early age by her teacher's skill and expertise:
'They always had good stories to tell you and a nice picture to show
you at the end.' She was also impressed by her Sunday School
teacher and by a Miss Hudson who taught her from 9 to 11-years-old
and got her through the scholarship:

'I used to look at them (the elementary school teachers) with
great awe and think how clever they were – I'd like to be as that.
They used to tell stories – history stories – I've always been mad
on stories. . . . When I was 9 to 11 I was in the junior school and I
had a most wonderful teacher and before the year was out I was
her right hand – 'cos that's why I suppose I liked her so much. She
used to choose me for everything and she would trust me to lock
up while she went off home and all that. I had her till I left to go to
Grammar School. And I thought what a lovely life she's got – she
was good – a good living woman – when I look back on it. And
when she got up to so many stories in a history book or note book
she'd used to put a paper in and before the history lesson I'd
always get it ready for her opened at the page . . . all her keys and
everything I knew and I always had to mind her handbag. When I
think of it my mother little knew what I used to do, nobody knew,
I used to be so proud when she left me in charge if she went out of
the room to mind the class and write down the name of anyone
who was naughty.'

'Were you a monitor?'

'Yes . . . we were supposed to be changed each week and she always used to work me in. I did like her though – I would have done anything for her. She was my ideal type of woman: she dressed well, her things were dainty and nice, clean – her shoes – and I thought I'd like to be like her when I grew up.'

It is interesting to notice how in this case the teachers clean, dainty clothes and ladylike manners and behaviour attracted the respondent to teaching.

She did so well in her Matriculation Exams that her headmistress suggested university:

'I was supposed to be going on to the University when I got up but as usual I was involved with a boyfriend . . . I got distinction when I matriculated and my headmistress said it would be such a waste if you don't go. But it meant another two or three years studying . . . I didn't think it was really fair on my mother. She'd got three other children – and I didn't think it was fair on myself – because I would be going up and down to a college in the East End and it was a horrible journey. I said to my mother I'd sooner be an ordinary teacher and go to college and only be two years there and get a job at once.'

Here we can see a recognition of the fact that further education often meant special sacrifices by the mothers not just fewer clothes, or outings for the girls themselves but the need to economise on all household expenditure to save money for their education.

When I asked about their parents' reaction to the idea of their daughters training to become elementary teachers, nearly all the respondents referred immediately to their mothers' part in encouraging them in this choice of career. The father's role was seen as much more passive. The fathers tended to be proud but silent about their daughters careers. Sometimes respondents had no idea at all about their father's reaction to their choice of work. Mrs Thomas for instance, only discovered that her father was really interested in her career when she read his prayer book years later and saw that he had added a note about her success in getting into the pupil teacher centre. In nearly all the interviews it was the mother who encouraged and listened to their daughter's problems when they were pupil teachers. When asked if their fathers had wanted them to become elementary teachers, most respondents suggested that 'it had all been left to Mother' and that fathers, although proud of their daughters becoming teachers, had not initiated the idea.

When schools had to be chosen it was the mother who searched for the one with a good reputation and who later visited the head and discussed their daughter's future and pressed for transfers to Higher Grade Schools or pupil teacher centres. This does not seem to have been merely that mothers had more free time than their husbands, but that they actively wanted their daughters to teach from an early age, as soon as the daughters showed signs of being fairly bright. Some mothers did not foresee their daughters specifically as teachers, but they all tended to have firm ideas that girls should be *trained* to do something and were thus open to the persuasion of the headmistresses that elementary teaching did not offer definite advantages over most other work open to girls. None of the mothers except one had been teachers themselves yet they were all convinced of the merits of elementary teaching, for their daughters. Most of the mothers had not been out to work prior to marriage, but had helped at home. The rest had worked in domestic service, in shops or as nurses. Only one had taught briefly at a small private school.

It is interesting to note that although the mothers of two informants had been nurses, they discouraged their daughters from taking up this profession. Miss Heron's mother, an ex-children's nurse, thought there was no security in that type of work and believed that hospital nursing was too strenuous physically and too gruelling emotionally.

It is not difficult to see why the mothers had a positive attitude towards elementary teaching as a career. It was probably the only womens' profession that they had had any close contact with. Most had been elementary school girls and as such had had a chance to see the advantages of teaching over the type of work they themselves did later. They must have realised that the hours of work were short, the job was clean and that elementary school mistresses could wear lady-like clothes. Also, when the mothers were at school in the period well before 1900, there had been much less talk of a marriage bar – they remembered their women teachers marrying and continuing to teach. This was a very different situation to that appertaining in the civil service. There the marriage bar was always rigidly enforced and even widows found it hard to re-enter the civil service again. One of the most important attractions in the eyes of the girls' mother was the security, of the pension offered by teaching, the civil service being the only other sphere of work which offered this to women. Miss Heron referred several times to her mothers passionate belief in the security of teaching.

'Of course why I chose to be a teacher, first of all, was that I was so devoted to children. I thought I'm going to do something with little children . . . I said I'm going to be a children's nurse and my mother said – No, have something that's more secure.'

'Did your mother know many women who became teachers?'

'Only those whom my elder sister got to know.'

'Then why did she think teaching was such a good job?'

'Well I mean mother was a very clever woman really. I mean she could see and understand quite a lot. She thought to be a teacher you'd got something solid – you can't be dismissed and it takes a pension and if you marry and then if you lost your husband or anything you could always go back to it – it was a thing that was yours, your teaching qualification. I suppose it was the same for trained nurses. Yes I suppose it was. But of course nurses need more physical strength . . . we had no idea of me being a hospital nurse.'

This extract shows us the essential difference between nursing and elementary teaching. While both were seen as channels of upward mobility for working class girls, nursing was seen as a tougher life needing a strong sense of vocation but elementary teaching was a job that a bright girl with any aptitude could cope with.

Miss Cox's mother had been the eldest child in the family for her own mother had married a widower with several young children and she became the 'family drudge'. Miss Cox's mother had been an intelligent girl and resented being restricted to this type of work at home. In contrast she had seen two of her cousins become elementary teachers and live away from home. Miss Cox remembered her mother admiring them because of their independence, their short working hours and long holidays and their greater status:

'She felt that they had got somewhere and she wanted to get somewhere through me which happened. My father died when I was six months out of college and my sister was at school. I went on through teaching.' (Miss Cox lived at home and became the sole breadwinner until her sister became a clerk in an insurance office.)

When I asked Miss Cox if her father had had anything to say about her becoming an elementary teacher she replied: 'No he left that to Mother'. It was Miss Cox's mother who took the initiative and asked to have her daughter moved to a Higher Grade School to prepare for a scholarship with a view to her becoming a teacher. Her mother was also active in insisting that Miss Cox went as a residential student so that they could enjoy the college facilities to the full although this was, of course, more costly. Her mother in fact paid the fees out of her own money, a family legacy which had just been left her, although her father was still alive at that time.

Mrs Barker's mother had never had a paid job but had helped at home before getting married. Similarly she was impressed by girls of her own age who became elementary teachers. Her mother was a Baptist whose best school friend, also a Baptist, went to Stockwell College (an undenominational College) and it became one of her mother's ambitions to send one of her own daughters there. In fact both Mrs Barker and her elder sister passed the scholarship exam and went on to Stockwell.

The emphasis on the pension made sense when some respondents referred to the fact that their mother's marriages were rather insecure and unhappy. Mrs Thomas described her father as unreliable and as a 'bit of a rover', and felt that this caused her mother to want her daughters to train for jobs that offered definite financial security:

'I was to get a job to bring a girl a pension because she had no money except what her husband would give her and she wanted her girl to have a pension – which I eventually did get.'

Mrs Thomas stressed that she felt she had had no particular wish to teach. The decision to send her to the pupil teacher centre was something that her mother and headmistress sorted out between them:

'There was never any discussion with me. I did what I was told
and of course you did have a sense of obedience in those days and
you did what you were told.'

Mothers often saw elementary teaching as a secure way for their
daughters to become economically independent, and to avoid the
necessity of marrying young. Indeed some teachers were in a strong
enough economic position not to marry at all.

Most of the respondents had left college before 1918 and thus had
had experience of living on pre-Burnham scale salaries i.e. about
35s per week in London. Those who lived at home with their
partners found that this was adequate, but those who lived in digs
(lodgings) were very short of money. Of the 13 respondents, 7 did
marry, 5 quite quickly after leaving training college and 2 much later
on. The ones who married quickly had often been unlucky in their
first job. They had suffered from bad teaching conditions and lack
of money. One respondent made it clear that she was very glad to
leave teaching and get married but those who weathered the first
years of low pay and lived at home were able, by the 1920s and
1930s, to have a comfortable standard of living as single women,
especially when they lived with sisters who were teachers or office
workers with a regular income.

Written sources suggest that the London School Board had not
required women teachers to resign on marriage and that the
London County Council continued this policy up to the 1920s. But
the London teachers I interviewed gave a very different account.
They were not always clear about exact dates but the general
impression was that married women were pulled in and out of
service at frequent intervals in the 1900–25 period. Most respondents remembered married women teaching them at London Board
Schools and Church Schools during the 1890s and 1900s, although
many of the teachers mentioned were in fact widows. But several
remembered women who married having to leave teaching *before*
the First World War and the ban being lifted during the war.
Women who married during the war could continue to teach after
1918, but new teachers after 1918 were sometimes forced to resign.

The respondents confirmed that by the 1920s the marriage bar
was imposed fairly strictly in most areas. Yet even in this period
when there was a large surplus of new college trained teachers, the
rule was sometimes relaxed. Mrs Fox described how she had to sign

an official declaration that she would resign on marriage when she started teaching in 1926 and when she married in 1928 she did have to resign. At first she did some supply work. Soon afterwards she was told by an official from the local educational office that she should apply for a permanent job at a village school in Sussex, which she did and was given the post. There were 96 other applicants and two single girls, both college trained, wrote to complain about her appointment because she was a married woman but the managers ignored the letters. Obviously local areas did relax the rule if it suited them. In this way the interviews helped to balance the official version and reflected variations in practice at local levels.

In the 1920s Miss Cox remembered her mother telling her that she would be a fool if she gave up teaching, with its security and pension, to marry. By this time a marriage bar was being introduced which often meant leaving the profession and forfeiting the pension. The interviews highlighted the possible economic advantages of remaining single if one was trained as an elementary teacher. It seems likely that school mistresses who married men such as clerks or male school teachers and tried to raise a family of several children on a small salary would have suffered a drop in their own standard of living. The respondents who remained single and enjoyed the sudden increase in wages after the new Burnham salary levels in 1918 (the starting wage for a trained school mistress rose from £90 pa to approximately £150 pa) found they could maintain a relatively high standard of living. They all remembered having good holidays and some of them could even afford to go abroad.

The interviews also revealed that size of family and the respondents position within it had influenced their chances of training as an elementary teacher. Several respondents felt that having older brothers who were already working had helped to make the prolonged training to become an elementary teacher more feasible. In fact one respondent felt that she would not have gone to training college in 1906, at least not as a residential student, if one of her brothers and a male cousin had not between them paid the fees. In other cases the burden of sending a daughter to training college on a small family income was eased by the fact that the number of children was small.

This was probably crucial in Miss Brook's case. Her father was an unskilled man but managed to send her to Stockwell, a residential college in 1922. Miss Brook felt that this was because she was one of only two children, her younger brother having failed his scholarship and left elementary school at 14 to be apprenticed as an engineer. In this particular case there was an extra incentive since both her parents had wanted to become elementary teachers themselves, but had been frustrated through lack of money and family support. Miss Brook felt, therefore, that they wanted to see their own thwarted ambitions fulfilled through her and they made every attempt to help her. She even went to Stockwell rather than the nearest college, Goldsmiths. the latter would have imposed a smaller burden on the family finances as she would have been eligible for a grant from her local Education Authority. She preferred Stockwell because her Secondary School favoured this College through a personal link: the Latin mistress's sister was Principal of Stockwell. But in any case Stockwell was thought to be more selective and refined than the newer co-educational Goldsmiths. Miss Brook summed up her parents attitude as:

> 'Let the girl have her way if we can. We can't do much for her but if she wants Stockwell we'll scroup and save so that she can go to Stockwell.'

Thus although her father's wage was only approximately 23s per week she was able to go to the college of her choice and her father paid the fees, £75 in the first year and £45 in the second year. Naturally enough she described having far less pocket money than the other girls.

Mrs Dublin, whose father was a compositor, is one of the few respondent's who came from a really large family. She was the eldest of eight, all of whom survived. She made the point that she felt it was very unusual, indeed, as one of such a large family to have been able to go to Goldsmiths in 1907. She emphasised that her family had not considered the idea of her becoming an elementary teacher until it was suggested by a teacher who gave her private piano lessons and whose own daughter was already at training college. Mrs Dublin sensed that this lady feared that her promising pupil might be pushed into a job merely to earn money or be kept at home to help with the little ones, so she offered to take her down to the pupil teacher centre and enrol her. In fact Mrs Dublin's mother took on this job willingly. In this case Mrs Dublin had two younger brothers who were earning money as clerks by the time she was to go to training college and this eased the financial situation.

Mrs Scott, born in 1895 in Lewisham, had a father who was a partner in a firm running a big tailors shop in Piccadilly. Her childhood was happy and comfortable and there were no financial problems as far as she knew. But on the sudden death of her father, when she was about 15, everything changed and there was very little money. She describes how her mother had to take up private nursing to earn money to keep her two daughters at school. The girls went into lodgings while she was nursing. Mrs Scott had always wanted to teach but now the idea of university was impossible. Instead the headmistress suggested she sat the Civil Service Exam but she failed to pass high enough up the list. The head offered her the only thing left, a bursary and the chance to become an elementary teacher. It is interesting that Mrs Scott herself was overjoyed at this prospect, to her it was infinitely preferable to the civil service. After being a student teacher for one year she went as a day student to Avery Hill College. She lived in digs rather than at a College hostel in order to save money, relying on a small government grant and money from her mother. She was desparately short financially and had to keep out of sports and social activities because she had no pocket money.

Miss Marsden whose father was a clerk at the Woolwich Arsenal attended Blackheath High School as a scholarship girl and at 16 her headmistress tried to persuade her to prepare for university but she rejected the idea of staying two more years at school followed by three more years of study at university. The reason she gives was the financial burden on the family. On the other hand it is interesting that this type of family felt it could afford to keep her elder sister at home without a job until she was 27. Miss Marsden also said that there was no pressure on her to work; she could have done the same as her sister, but she chose not to. This interview suggests that middle-class families were likely to prefer to keep their daughters at home rather than allow them to go away to a residential college. Miss Marsden describes her disappointment when her mother refused to let her go to Saffron Waldron College, and she was forced to go to Goldsmiths as a day student.

At first glance the fees for training college do not look very high. Indeed when one considers that some colleges in the 1900s were only charging £25 pa for two years board, lodging and training they seem to be providing excellent value for money. But these fees often had to be found in lump sums and there were also the holiday periods to allow for, plus the cost of clothes and pocket money. The interview with Mrs Brown makes it clear that even a skilled draughtsman like her father earning £3 per week, found it a financial strain to send two of his daughters to training college in 1911. But her two older brothers had left home and were earning and this left only four children at home. She and her stepsister went to college at the same time. As day students they each received a grant of £18 pa but this did not by any means cover the family's expenditure:

'It was very good of him. There were the two of us. And certainly we bought our own clothes. Paid out our own college expenses. We still lived at home. He had to feed two of us. Quite an item in those days'.

Mrs Brown emphasises the fact that the £18 grant could not cover clothes, general expenses and food. In other words board and lodging was provided free of cost by their father for the two years they were at College. Mrs Brown explained that she got £6 per term but that 30s had to go on compulsory college lunches and then books, travelling expenses and pocket money had to come out of the £4 10s that remained. She remembered how they always walked to college and shared books whenever possible to make this money last longer.

The interviews revealed that few respondents had any image of training college life before they became students. Only those with sisters or cousins already there seemed to have had any sense of what it would be like. When they chose which training college to apply to they relied on the advice of their old elementary teachers or the teachers at the schools where they were pupil teachers or student teachers. The distance in the relationship between pupil teachers and the ordinary staff of the school often prevented them from asking about the situation generally at training college. From the interviews, residential colleges do not seem to have been chosen by girls as a way of escaping from the restrictions of home for the new experience of living in a student community and only one respondent mentioned looking forward to the boarding-school type of experience offered by living in college.

The study of the respondents' family background, emphasised

how important it was to have some financial stability to be able to become a trained teacher. At the same time there were signs that an element of financial insecurity, for example where the father's character or income was seen as unreliable, actually encouraged daughters to enter the relative safety of elementary teaching, with its promise of economic independence for a single woman after a few years of teaching (when several increments had been accumulated) and a pension in old age. Equally the interviews showed that the marriage bar was never absolute even in the 1920s. It was possible for a married woman to do supply teaching and we have seen how, in certain areas, they could still get permanent posts.

Elementary teaching was one of the few jobs which offered married women short hours and relatively good pay. Respondents who returned to teaching after having several children, stressed how their salary was an important supplement to the family budget. All the respondents emphasised that elementary teaching offered security to women who were widows for their re-entry at this level of teaching was fairly easy. Interviews also revealed that, in many cases, mothers played a vital role in either stressing these advantages to their daughters, or else in simply making the choice for them possibly in consultation with the Headmistress and presenting the girls with the *fait accompli*.

Some distinction can be made between the general situation of working-class girls and on the other hand, those from lower middle-class homes when recruited into elementary teaching. Bright working class girls had very few careers open to them: the lowest ranks of nursing or elementary office work. Lower middle-class girls were also limited to nursing, teaching or office work but they had a wider range of work within each of these spheres. They could afford to train as Norland nurses or have to have private tuition for the civil service exams. They had access to a greater variety of teaching jobs, for example, they could teach Domestic Science or Physical Training, subjects which were taught at more expensive private colleges. Lower middle-class girls with enough money and intelligence often aimed to teach in Girl's High Schools or in County Secondary Schools. For some lower middle-class girls there was also the choice of staying at home and not taking a job at all. While elementary teaching offered working-class girls a real rise in social position there was less to be gained, in terms of social prestige, by lower middle-class girls who became elementary teachers.

Furthermore, the lower middle-class girl had not normally attended a public school, at least during the early period up to 1914, so that parents were likely to want a sign of a *real* vocation for elementary teaching in their daughters before letting them start in the somewhat alien environment of state schools. However, as has been shown, the Higher Grade School could help to bridge the gap for girls. Thus the interviews tended to show that respondents from lower middle-class homes saw their own sense of vocation as the crucial factor in choosing to become elementary teachers and the influence of parents and teachers as having less influence.

Mrs Scott is a good example of a middle class girl who wanted to teach at all costs. She needed a strong sense of vocation to persevere and train against heavy odds with very little money. When asked if she was ever tempted to stop training to become a secretary and earn some money she replied:

'I never even thought what I was going to earn that didn't come into it . . . to begin with there were very few things women could do in the professional way, but even that didn't affect me – that is what you realize looking back – lady doctors were just beginning, breaking in: there was the civil service or there was teaching.'

'That was the choice for the middle-class girl?'

'Yes but I wasn't influenced in any way. I just wanted to be . . . I persisted in wanting to be in spite of things that happened and of course never regretted it . . . I could have done with more money but I never thought about it. When I started I got £90 a year.' (1915)

This is not to suggest that working-class respondents lacked a sense of vocation but rather they laid stress on it. Many had had a strong desire to teach and work with children. And it would be wrong to suggest that working-class girls were pressurised into this career *against their wishes*, by ambitious mothers who were looking for a way of edging their daughters, and indirectly themselves, up the social scale. Nevertheless, if a working-class girl were bright it was almost automatically assumed that she should try being a pupil teacher or student teacher. Unless her personality or health was unsuited to teaching, there was immense pressure from teachers and mothers to get started in elementary teaching.

Given the apparently heavily restricted range of possibilities open to these types of girls, it is important to carefully analyse alternatives and assess elementary teaching against them. It was clear that respondents rated nursing on a par with elementary teaching. In fact several of their sisters did take up nursing. But leaving aside the need for a special vocation, nursing presented some additional problems. Several respondents referred to the late age when training began for nurses, 18 or 21. For instance, Miss Heron had begun her training as a pupil teacher when she was 15 in 1903. Had she wanted to become a hospital nurse she would have had to find a fill-in job for at least three, and possibly six years. There were no schemes to bridge the gap between the end of a scholarship at 16 and the start of hospital training at 18. By 1907 however, the future elementary teacher could have free secondary education up to 17 years, then a year as a student teacher, followed by two years at College and be fully trained by 20.

However, there were other reasons for avoiding nursing. Some respondents had stressed how they had wanted to live a normal family life at home while training and afterwards when they were actually teaching. This was impossible for the hospital nurse. Elementary teaching offered girls the chance of a fair wage and some prospect of promotion, in the long run, without sacrificing their chance of a home life. Like girls in offices, their salary would go much further if they lived at home; their food was likely to be better and there were extras such as free washing and sewing.

It also seems that respondents were very dependent on their homes for social activities. The schools in which they taught often provided them with a few social contacts of their own age, some remembered being the only young member of the staff. Small schools employed only a limited staff and even the large board schools were split into three sections with little contact between the staff in the infants, the girls and boys sections thus the range of friends amongst the staff was quite restricted. Training college friends were usually dispersed over a fairly wide area and contact was kept up mainly by correspondence. Generally therefore, the respondents depended on local ex-schoolfriends, family friends and relatives as their main social group. Church societies which required little financial outlay were often the central pivot of their social lives with tennis and rambling clubs, weekly dances in the church hall. Thus to move away from home into digs and teach at a school where

there were no other young teachers, would have meant considerable isolation.[5]

In the first few years after training college when a teacher's salary
was still quite low, home offered a cheap and more secure social life.
The interviews indicate that moving away from home was not
something necessarily to be longed for by single girls between 1900
and 1925. The accommodation available to young women on
limited wages was discouraging. Working-class girls in particular
who were still close to the tradition of domestic service which had
forced them to leave home at a very early age, were not tempted to
voluntarily moving away from their families.

Office work was the sphere most often mentioned as the possible
alternative to elementary teaching. Some of the respondents
seriously toyed with the idea of doing office jobs, and many of their
sisters did take it up. Certainly the higher grades of the civil service
compared favourably on most points with elementary teaching.
Posts were secure, pay was reasonable, hours were fairly short, the
work was clean while it was possible to live at home. The civil
service was less attractive in that the marriage bar was rigidly
imposed yet competition to get into the service was very great.
Many schools did not prepare girls for these exams and it was
necessary to take a special course either full time or in the evenings.
The problem was that many girls never finished their courses but got
sidetracked into ordinary office work, although, of course, work in
the commercial sector did not have the same security as civil service
or local government positions.

Respondents were asked about domestic service and shopwork
mainly to assess the attitude of their families to such work. As
expected, the respondents, like most secondary schoolgirls, felt that
this type of work was beneath them, but it was interesting to find
that it was also thought to be unsuitable for other girls in their
family, even those who had failed the scholarship and did not seem
to like school. But even these girls had had a better than average
education at Higher Grade or Central Schools and domestic service
and shopwork were not considered good enough for them. Miss
Lomax described how her sister felt domestic service and shopwork
was out of the question:

'Did she choose to become a typist?'

'I don't think there was much else a person could do apart from going into homes – domestic work – which of course she wouldn't, it wouldn't have come into our particular range. It would usually be children without more than average ability would go into homes and sometimes be very well trained for domestic work. They could rise to nice families. I suppose the only thing was shorthand typing and I suppose her own friends would nearly all do that.'

Miss Lomax described how her sister earned very little while training as a shorthand-typist with a lady who ran an office in the West End. It was really pocket money and she was totally dependent on her parents for everything else. Domestic service was obviously left to girls from families who could not afford to feed a growing girl and Miss Lomax, whose father was a fireman, prided itself on not being one of this class. Of the three girls in the family, two became elementary teachers.

Although conditions for shop assistants had improved they still worked long hours and they were sometimes expected to live in. Miss Brook felt that shopwork compared badly with elementary school teaching:

'You earned quite good money as an elementary teacher?'

'Oh yes . . . for a young woman . . . The only other alternative was domestic work and shops . . . less money and much harder hours on the whole – longer hours and more restrictions . . . shop girls lived in nearly till 1930. Some were living in when World War 2 broke out.'

The interviews confirmed that it was mainly lower-middle-class girls rather than girls of the well-to-do or professional middle classes who were increasingly entering elementary teaching. When asked about the social background of other students at their colleges, respondents confirmed that there were very few daughters of clergymen or doctors. They suggested that girls of this type were still either expected to live at home after leaving school or, if they were very bright, to go to university or enter the professions. But clearly university fees were prohibitive for the clerk or small business man's daughter. Instead they turned to elementary training colleges for higher-education and in the longer term as a way of becoming self-supporting. Some well-to-do girls did not go into elementary teaching because of a sudden collapse of their family finances (e.g. death of father), but in the period up to 1920 such girls were likely to have a real vocation to teach in addition to financial need which helped them to brave this new sphere of work. The majority of girls from the solid middle class and fairly prosperous homes probably continued to see the conditions of elementary teaching as unattractive at least up to the end of the First World War. By the 1920s a new era was beginning for elementary teaching which began to attract middle class girls who had no strong vocation to teach. This suggests that by this time, elementary teaching, with its increased salary, had become a much more generally accepted job for a middle class girl and more women were seeking to work for a salary rather than stay at home.

The interviews serve to show how far the situation had changed by the early twentieth century from the often bleak picture of overworked pupil teachers as presented in the *Report on the Pupil Teacher System* in 1898. After the new student teacher system was established in 1907, very few of the respondents felt they had been overworked as trainee teachers, they now remained at secondary school till they were 17 years old and had only one year of actual teaching and there were regulations limiting the student teachers from taking full responsibility for a class until their final term. However, it is probable that the traditional image of the apprentice teacher in elementary schools as overworked and overstrained was popularly held, for at least another decade, especially by middle class parents who had little first hand experience of these schools. Only by the 1920s was this old image dying out among the prosperous middle classes.

The interviews also helped to balance the theories which had been put forward in the 1870s by feminist propagandists like Louisa Hubbard. Their writing suggests that girls who went to training college wanted to work away from home to be independent, longing to be their own boss in a small village school, living in their own school house in contrast to the governess who usually lived with her employer, or else to enjoy the freedom of living in lodgings in a big town. This probably bore little relation to the real situation of most girls, certainly to the experiences of the respondents between 1900 and 1925. They rather emphasised practicalities. They lived at home because their salaries went further that way, and because most of them preferred the security of their own families to the freedom but potential loneliness of being in digs.

Oral material for these interviews has been invaluable as a way of ascertaining girls' motives for choosing elementary teaching as a career. It could also be used to compare the situation of women teaching in rural areas and smaller towns. It might well turn out that the lower middle-class girl who entered elementary teaching in the 1900s was a largely urban phenomenon. Efficient Higher Grade Schools, well-run pupil-teacher centres and non-residential training facilities were all on offer in urban areas which may account for the undoubted increase in recruitment of lower middle-class girls in the 30 years or so between 1890 and 1920, although one might suggest that the very presence of these facilities indicates a demand already created by other factors. The lively memories of this small group of London women give a vivid confirmation to the fact that from the end of the nineteenth century, elementary teaching was becoming part of the widening opportunities for middle-class women to earn an income through respectable if not highly prestigious work.

Notes

1. There are many references to pupil teachers being overworked in the *Pupil Teacher Report 1898*. The problem was that many schools were understaffed and thus pupil teachers were used as full time teachers with full responsibility for their classes. This was against the regulations but it often happened, particularly in poor rural areas. The principals and teachers of some pupil teacher centres felt that adolescent girls in particular suffered from anaemia through having to study and teach as well as undertaking domestic tasks at home. By 1907 this half-time system was fading and most urban areas adopted the student teacher system whereby the future teacher was a full time pupil at secondary school till 17. This obviously eased the strain for these later trainee teachers.

2. An exam had been set in 1858 to test the suitability of middle class girls as candidates for training college. Most of the girls failed to pass this preliminary exam. The Taunton Commission a few years later revealed the full extent of the deficiencies of the private schools attended by middle-class girls.

3. Louisa Hubbard's pamphlet *Elementary Teaching for Ladies* (1871, price 3d) was widely circulated and the idea of recruiting middle-class girls into elementary teaching was often discussed in the national press,

by local school boards and by education magazines. Kay Shuttleworth supported the campaign and suggested using a disused mens' college at Chichester as the new training college for ladies. The students at this Bishop Otter College were to come from genteel homes, i.e. daughters of clergymen and professional men. This college would prepare girls who had not had the advantage of being pupil teachers to pass the examinations necessary to gain a government subsidised place at the college with a view to becoming a fully qualified elementary teacher.

4. National statistics on the social origins of those gaining bursaries in England and Wales between 1909 and 1911 indicate that labourers' daughters formed only 3.2 per cent of girls holding bursaries. Many rural areas carried on the old pupil teacher system. Girls did two or three years pupil teaching and then became provisional teachers and took their acting teacher exams. Going to Training Colleges was considered a luxury beyond the pockets of most rural teachers.

5. For a portrait of a teacher in this situation, see the autobiography of Helen Corke who taught at an elementary school in Croydon. One of the friends she did make was D. H. Lawrence when he was teaching in a boys school in the town. Helen Corke, *In Our Infancy*, 1975.

6 'A Cissy Job for Men; a Nice Job for Girls': Women Shorthand Typists in London, 1900–39

TERESA DAVY

In the late 1880s the Civil Service began to employ female clerks, keeping them secluded from other departments and feeding them through a hatch in the wall. At this time the early entrants were women with middle and lower middle-class backgrounds, relatively well educated and who had been forced to prove that they needed employment. These early clerks worked as copyists and typists producing letters or forms and were usually in the lower grades of office work.

It was during the 1880s that the combination of shorthand with typewriting began. Before this time, shorthand was a skill included in a list of technical occupations and was not solely linked with a commercial career. With the competition of new entrants into office work due to greater educational opportunities and the influx of foreign clerks with good commercial education, shorthand became a skill which, it was hoped, would enhance the status of the clerk. It was a skill which could be acquired by both men and women, and 'with Pitman's Shorthand emerging in the late 1880s as the premier system', shorthand writers 'seeking to propagandise their skills, established associations and journals throughout the country'.[1] The most important of these societies were the Phonetic Shorthand Writers' Association (1872) and the Incorporated Phonographic Society (1891). The two societies merged in 1894 to form the National Society of Shorthand Teachers.

The first typewriters were introduced into the office in the same decade, the 1880s, and it was during this period that the combination of the two skills began. It has often been stated that when typewriters were introduced they were solely the preserve of women. This is not strictly true, as there were some male typists. However, from its inception, women were particularly encouraged to learn the skill. The prospectus of the Pitman's Metropolitan School wrote in 1893:

> Ladies will find Shorthand and Typewriting offer an occupation in which they are eminently qualified to excel. Ladies are now largely employed as amanuenses and private secretaries, and in the present acute struggle for existence, girls would do much better by learning Shorthand and Typewriting (by which, when proficient, they could earn a competency), than in acquiring mechanical dexterity on the piano, which only pays those who have great musical taste and ability, or in endeavouring to earn a living as governesses without having been specially trained in the work.[2]

During the first decade of this century, there were men and women typists and shorthand writers. As more women entered the occupation however, they tended to take the jobs as shorthand typists, leaving male clerks to perform other functions. A woman starting work in 1905 explained one feature of this transition in her work for a small office connected to a gentleman's outfitters in the City of London. When she started work she had very little to do, but gradually the male copyists handed over their work to her:

> 'Well, I suppose they did more and they'd been used to writing their own letters. You see they weren't used to having a typist. So gradually the letters increased and then I got all the counting house letters.'

As women entered the Civil Service they also took over the functions of the male copyists. Typewriting was a new occupation, but comparability could be made with older clerical functions. Although there were men working as typists and shorthand writers, they had different reasons for learning the skills. With the threat of an oversupply of clerks at the end of the century, male clerks began to learn extra skills, skills which were a means to the end of job mobility. Women, on the other hand, tended to learn the skills as an end in themselves. The Pitman's School prospectus of 1905 recommended that both men and women should have a knowledge of English grammar and composition, arithmetic, shorthand, typewriting, business training and, whenever possible, bookkeeping. 'In the case of Ladies, Typewriting is really compulsory, as it is rarely that a Lady's handwriting is considered suitable, without special training, for business purposes.'

This was perhaps a justification, not so much of women's disabilities, but of what was going on in the clerical labour market. At the end of the nineteenth century there were fears that women's entry into offices would see the disappearance of the male clerk. The outcry took the form of fears for the loss of femininity with cartoons portraying women in farcical masculine roles. Underlying this was, however, a fear that women would put the male breadwinner out of work and generally reduce the salaries of clerical workers.

By the beginning of the century these anxieties had subsided. Ultimately women were entering *new* occupations which were created by the changing economy and the changes in office organisation, leaving men to enter other new careers which were also being created by the specialisation of offices: cost accountants, office managers, commercial travellers and salesmen. Moreover, women were a cheap form of labour, and even if the small offices did not entirely change their organisation, they could cut costs by employing female shorthand-typists and typists. As fears about women's entry were allayed, a rationale was built up showing that office work was women's 'natural sphere'. The typewriter was analogous to the piano and suitable for female fingers. Women, it was said, did not have the characteristics of initiative and strong judgement; they were naturally neat, precise, efficient and careful and were eminently suited for the job as shorthand-typists. Since many characteristics of the female shorthand-typists had similarities to the male copyists and correspondence clerks, the occupation underwent a 'feminisation' process, both in its composition and in the ideology which encompassed it. The job involved little decision making, was often methodical and required neatness and precision, traits easily associated with women.

Office work had many advantages for women seeking employment in the first decade of the twentieth century. It was clean, respectable and required a certain amount of specialised education. For lower-middle-class women, in particular, it had the appeal of being a viable alternative to the restricting personal service of the governess or dubious status of shop keeping. Moreover, the strict discipline and theoretical sexual segregation, (although for practical reasons could not be completely enforced), met with parental approval. For women from working-class backgrounds who were able to take advantage of the new opportunities in education, it was a welcome alternative to the confines of domestic service, dressmaking and factory work. With the mixture of members from different social backgrounds it was a 'nice job' for a girl to do.

Although women were increasingly using the skills of shorthand and typewriting, there were various grades of work developing. There were girls with superior education, both secondary and commercial, proficient in shorthand, typewriting and business practice, who worked as secretaries for one man or as shorthand typists for more than one person. Secondly, there were girls proficient in typewriting and copying who could be found in all the better class typewriting offices and business houses. Thirdly, there were the girls with no secondary or commercial education, who entered office work straight from elementary school and were taught typewriting at work. It is important to differentiate between the different types of work in order to make any comment about the class composition of the occupation and the educational background of its work force.

There appears to be some confusion about the class composition of female clerks at this time. On the one hand, there is the assertion that the early pioneers were women from middle and lower-middle-class backgrounds. On the other, it is asserted that the great mass of female clerks came directly from elementary school with little initial commercial education. This confusion derives from misunderstanding the grades of work that existed. When looking at the 40 years as a whole there appears to be a gradual increase of women whose fathers were skilled, semi-skilled or unskilled manual workers, and a slight decline of women whose fathers were in the lower-middle-class: i.e. lower professionals, small-businessmen, lower management, office workers, salesmen and commercial travellers.

It would appear that commercial education depended on basic education acquired at elementary or secondary school and the ability to pay. The fees were too expensive for many working-class families and many of the women who attained the better jobs were from higher social origins. Many of the working-class entrants went into offices straight from school at this time, although the position of the family cycle would have been important, and parents less dependent on their daughter's income would have been able to allow extra time and expenditure for training.

Office organisation and the functions the shorthand typist performed were extremely varied and the particularism of the nineteenth century was not as entirely eroded as some commentators would like to believe. Within the Civil Service, the office organisation was departmentalised and the work was graded. However, in the small offices in the City, the shorthand typist might be in a room with other typists, sitting at a trestle-table and supervised by a woman; or she might be carefully secluded in a small office connected to a warehouse, the only woman in a male workforce. Indeed, it is a major trend during the forty years of this study that a division arose between the shorthand typists in the Civil Service and the shorthand-typists in the private sector. The Civil Service was a bureaucratic organisation with standardised work functions and salaries, whereas in the private sector, remuneration varied and work functions were created by the particular office or boss. Related to these organisational differences, Civil Service clerks tended to unionise, whereas unionisation was almost non-existent in other offices.

The fact that the women were entering new jobs at the lower end of the clerical market could be a justification for lower rates of pay. However, as Holcombe points out, where comparability could be made this argument does not hold:

> Second Division male clerks received salaries of £80–£350, women clerks, at the time of their establishment, received only £65–£150. Also, women typists were paid at much lower rates than men and boy copyists they replaced. By 1914 women typists received 20s–26s weekly or roughly £52–£68 yearly, and shorthand-typists 28s–30s a week or about £72–£78 a year, compared with men typists in one department receiving £3–£4 a week, or £156–£208 a year, at piece rate and men shorthand-writers, in various departments earning £104–£300 yearly.[3]

Although there was a demand for competent typists; they were still paid less than their male counterparts indicating that non-market forces were predominant.

Women's wages were based on the 'pin money' idea. Young women in particular were considered as being subsidised by husbands or fathers. This particularly incensed some of the first female clerical unions. The Association of Women Clerks and Secretaries often showed the expenditure of a female worker, taking into account board and lodging. They often emphasised the middle-class woman living away from home in a hostel, although the majority were living with parents and contributing to the family wage.

The shorthand typist lived a rather secluded life at work, often working on her own and separated from other workers. She worked overtime on demand, receiving no extra pay. Offices were often badly constructed and ventilated with little legislative protection of their conditions. Many of these women were destined to stay shorthand typists because lack of marriage opportunities and occupational advancement, except in terms of their own sphere of work and remuneration. On the other hand, in comparison to other female workers, the shorthand typist was in a fairly privileged position. At a time when many women needed employment, she set herself apart from the less educated workforce, and had freedom and status never experienced by the governess or school teacher. She went to work dressed in a flannel or serge suit. The top shorthand typist or secretary distinguished herself through dress from the typist, but not, on the other hand, to be mistaken for the 'Society' woman. She enjoyed two weeks paid holiday, a luxury not introduced to manual work until 1938.

The First World War economy created more opportunities for women in offices, not only as shorthand typists, but in higher positions which had not been available before the war. On the whole however, these opportunities were temporary and with demobilisation of the forces, expansion ceased. For the next 20 years there was a period of consolidation of women in the lower echelons of the clerical hierarchy as bars, formal and informal set a ceiling on women's promotion.

Looking at the period in closer detail, we see that when the First World War broke out, there was an initial slump in clerical work, particularly in the commercial sector. However, as businesses adapted to war conditions and new ministries opened in the Civil Service, women were needed to replace the men who had joined the armed forces. In London the number of female clerks grew from 25 per cent to 34 per cent in the public service and from 20 per cent to 44 per cent in the private sector. The new demand for female labour also had an effect of raising salaries. There were however, two trends existing at this time. On the one hand, women were proving that they were able to take on responsible jobs. On the other, there was always the assumption that this was temporary work.

Interview material is important in showing these diverse effects of the First World War and can higlight certain historical events. Mrs H. pointed out that women were employed in the Swansea Post Office on a temporary basis for the duration of the war. When the men returned she was the only woman whose services were retained because she was doing shorthand and typewriting. The other women had been doing other clerical functions. A draughtswoman, Mrs T, also recalled that there were men doing typewriting before the war, but when they returned to the Middlesbrough Railway Company, they refused to do 'women's work' which was considered 'sissy'.

> 'And of course, as you see as the men came back we were supposed to be redundant, you see to move out when the men came. But the men came back and they saw girls doing their jobs, so they weren't going to do typing, it was a "sissy" job for them.'
>
> *'Is that how they felt about it?'*
>
> 'Yes. So of course we kept our jobs, and I think that's how it grew for women, more and more came in.'

The war also saw the last vestiges of the male typist and shorthand writer. Although women temporary clerks were disposed of in the Civil Service, the female typists and shorthand typists tended to keep their jobs. When the men returned they no longer took these positions.

It has been argued that the existence of women who would never marry did not necessarily create greater opportunities for women in the clerical hierarchy. Instead recruitment and functions were based on the assumption that women would marry and used as a justification for keeping them in the lower positions and paying them less. In addition, any comparability between men's and women's work had vanished during the First World War. This view was strengthened by general trends at the beginning of the 1930s when women entering the labour market had more opportunities to marry. The effects of male war losses had decreased and more marriages were being celebrated and at a younger age, particularly after 1933 when the economy was making a recovery. This situation effectively defined women's position in the labour market for the next ten years. Employers reinforced the status quo and most women saw work as a stop-gap between school and marriage.

During the 1920s and 1930s there were several trends in the London economy which affected women's opportunities. Between 1921 and 1931 female clerks only grew by 1 per cent, however, comparing the figures for the years 1911–31, female workers grew to represent nearly half of all clerical workers in London. The small percentage rise between 1921 and 1931 was due to the large participation of women in 1921, a contraction of opportunities for the next ten years, and the tendency to rationalise office organisation.

Using oral evidence, it was found that most of the shorthand-typists working in the 1920s and 1930s came from lower-middle-class backgrounds, their father's being small businessmen or clerks. There were some representatives from working class backgrounds and a proportion of shorthand-typists whose fathers and mothers had been domestic servants. It is important to look at the mother's occupation before marriage, as this can often indicate the career she will help to choose for her daughter. Women working as domestic servants had been in an environment where respectability and education were important. Their daughters working as clerks would therefore enhance the status of the family.

It is argued that the class background of an occupation will ultimately determine its status.[4] Thus while clerical work in the nineteenth century had a high status because of its middle class composition, it has been argued that clerical work lost its status because it was gradually becoming an occupation of the working class. The outcry during the first decade of the twentieth century concerning standards, was not merely about professional status, but also a fear about the entry of young people from the working class.

The fear that clerical work would lose its respectability was based on the assumption that it would ultimately take the characteristics of manual work. It does however appear that although there were more working-class entrants, they did not take with them the values of the worker in manual labour, but of the class above them. It is interesting to look at the attitudes of women who were clerical workers during the thirties, to see how they viewed their status in relation to manual occupations. Women interviewed set themselves apart from manual workers because of their education and their superior speech:

> '. . . it was more the middle-class people or at any rate upper lower-class people, partly because of the speech defect. You see you had to answer the telephone . . . I never thought of myself as middle class – I was more referred to as upper lower class. Middle class is more the type of person whose sons went to public school, whereas in our case they mainly went to grammar school. So it was about the grammar school level that got jobs in offices.'

Most companies wanted to know the parent's background and with greater competition for clerical posts, many companies could insist on grammar school educated clerks. It is therefore argued that although there was a gradual increase of working class entrants, the respectability and status of the job was not lost. Although the occupation of shorthand-typists was not a profession, the educational differentials – either secondary or commercial – set it apart from manual work. Moreover the actual functions performed by the shorthand typist were respectable. She worked in close proximity to authority and the relationship between herself and her boss was personal. It was a sharp contrast to the manual labourer who worked in an impersonal environment and whose identification was with her fellow worker as opposed to the decision-maker.

In saying that shorthand typists had a higher status than manual workers, it is interesting to see what alternative occupation a girl might have considered, and indeed, why office work was chosen. It must be stressed that girls of 14 or 15 had little idea about the labour market and their occupations were usually chosen by their parents or relatives. From interviews it was found that the most popular alternative career was elementary-school teaching. Some women stated that they would liked to have been teachers, and it became clear that family income and parental influence played a major part in choosing the occupation. In some cases it was obvious that the extra expenditure needed for training after secondary education was not available and office work seemed to be the obvious choice after teaching. There were however women who wanted to be shorthand typists. It was something new and seemed more fashionable than the image of the school marm:

'My mother wanted me to be a teacher. But oh no I was kind of head-strong. I couldn't imagine myself being a teacher, you know, I thought it was a dreadful thing to do. . . .'

'You said that your mother wanted you to be a teacher, why did you decide not to do teaching and why did you decide to do office work?'

'Just, I fancied it. I think . . . you see at the time it was new to women. There were no typists, they were all men. But of course they went to the war you see.'

Another respondent pointed out that she would have liked to have become a teacher, but it was out of the question because her mother was a widow. Her headmistress pointed out the benefits of shorthand and typewriting, and she was able to do her training while still at school.

* * *

It was the personal relationship with her boss which gave the shorthand typist her respectability. She was, in a sense, associated with authority although she never actually wielded it. The mystification of job functions and the linking of a job to the particular boss, made her feel unique and important. However, a shorthand typist knew she was not indispensible. Most shorthand typists and secretaries during their training at college, would learn how to answer the telephone, to dress correctly and to be quiet and unassuming, supportive rather than assertive.

The shorthand typist's status could also be enhanced by being promoted to work for an important member of the company. Here, it was not so much that the functions of the job changed, but the status of the shorthand typist was raised by virtue of her boss' status within the company. One woman received this type of promotion when she was working in an electrical company in London in the early-1930s:

'When you changed from the typing pool to working for the Managing Director's son, did you see any difference in the type of work you were doing?'

'Well it was a little more important, you know, because he wrote more to companies about the work. The others (I worked for an accounts department and another department) I worked for when I was still in the pool – that was the department that sold the gas-mantles, and, you know, "We have today delivered 2000 mantles", or whatever it would have been.'

'Did you have to do any other work besides shorthand and typing?'

'Not at that time, no, never.'

'Not even for the Managing Director's son?'

'No. We didn't even have to answer the telephone.'

Another woman, commenting on the status of the shorthand typist's relationship to the boss' position in the company said:

'. . . all I can say is that when the particular people they worked for perhaps got promoted, they got promoted with them.'

In the private sector a rather haphazard system of remuneration and wage negotiation existed, which was strictly based on experience or responsibility. Women would often spend years in one company without getting recognition of their duties and without the backing of a union to support their claims. One woman explained her methods of getting a salary rise to which she felt she was entitled:

'I stayed there until about 1934 and I thought I'd go and ask for a rise. I hadn't had a rise since the depression business. And I went and asked for a rise and I was too shy to go and ask for a rise straight out and I told them I'd have to leave because I'd been offered a job with more money (which was a lie, you see). And they said, "Well how much money are you getting?," and I thought, "Oh God, what shall I say," I said talking to myself. So just out of the blue, I said, "£2 7s 6d," I said, And so the boss said, "Alright Miss Tobias, go away and we'll think about it." So I went back to my desk and he sent for me an hour later and he said,

"We'll make your money up to £2 7s 6d". So I thought for a minute and I said, "No". I said that won't do, I said, because I can see I'll have to work here another five years and I'll have to threaten you with another job before you give me another rise. I said, "I've made my mind up to go, and I'm going." Because I had no job to go to, I might tell you . . . well I thought I ought to get more money, that's all. Because by this time – how old would I have been? 22 – And I was only earning 33s 10d a week, you know. And I felt that I was worth more, apart from anything else.'

There were several ways a shorthand typist got promoted. The most obvious was to move to another organisation to get a higher salary. Alternatively, as already mentioned, it was a form of promotion if her boss got promoted or if the shorthand-typist was promoted in the same company by carrying out more important functions, usually based on less shorthand and typewriting and an increase in duties related to her boss' activities. There were also the more prestigious establishments to work in. Central and local government, insurance and banking carried higher status than industrial or commercial companies. The latter tended to pay less, and there might be links with manual work as offices were sometimes housed in the same building as a warehouse or engineering plant.

The size of the company was also linked to promotional opportunities. Respondents interviewed who worked in small commercial offices commented that there was more scope for promotion in a large company of the civil service. However, it was not necessarily the case that a shorthand-typist would want to move to one of these larger organisations. Many worked in small offices until they married. The relationship built up between themselves and their bosses was often a break against advancement but felt to be a form of security and pleasant work environment. Moreover, the fact that there were few opportunities of rising above the position of shorthand typist or secretary meant that once they had found a suitable position, there was little motivation to move on:

'I mean I was fortunate in the fact that I worked for one of the partners, but if you were a shorthand typist, you really stayed a shorthand typist, you didn't become a secretary, they were few and far between really. It's like if you were a clerk, you very rarely got on to anything else, you just stayed in that one position. You might have got a rise for being there that time, but you didn't get much promotion really at all. No, they weren't very good, the prospects really, I was fortunate that I worked for a partner.'

It could be argued that because women left employment when they married, this was the reason why they held jobs in 'watertight compartments', strictly separate and distinct from comparable men's grades'.[5] However, as has been argued for the earlier period, the characteristics of 'male' and 'female' clerical work evolved at a time when there were many women who would never marry. Women's employment was based on their cheapness and on the assumption that they would marry, even though it was not necessarily the reality. By the 1930s this rationale had more force behind it, and resentment was expressed if any woman took a job which was considered a 'male' job. By this time 'male' and 'female' jobs were more often defined and rigid. Women's work was seen as a stop-gap between school and marriage. Men needed advancement because they were future breadwinners. One woman interviewed, spoke about the resentment against her expressed by both male and female members of her office. She was an older woman who worked as the supervisor of a subscriptions department of a trade news-paper and also reported various social functions for the paper. The work was considered suitable for a man, and she was earning a 'man's' salary:

'You said that you were earning a man's wage?'

'That was a man's wage, £3 15s.'

'What was the average wage for a woman in an office at that time?'

'Well, should say about £3 would have been the limit, if she'd got a supervisory job. I was very much resented there because I was getting a man's wage. I was always being told I was getting a man's wage.'

'Who by?'

. . . by . . . people know. I mean somebody in the Accounts Department would tell somebody else. There was quite a big staff . . . I was in charge of all the female staff there whether they were in my department or not.'

'Did they resent you having a man's wage? Did the female resent having a man's wage?'

'Oh yes, course they did.'

'What about the men?'

'Well the men did, of course, everybody did: "A man ought to have the job, why has it been given to a woman."'

Women shorthand typists therefore had some promotional opportunities within their sphere of work, but they very rarely crossed over to other forms of work. Parallel with the development and changes in office work at the lower end of the ladder, was the increasing specialisation at the top, mostly taken by men. These positions required prolonged training and good qualifications which effectively blocked women's entry when combined with such social expectations.

Office hours and the overtime system remained similar in the later period. The shorthand typist usually worked at least an eight-hour day during the week, and about four hours on Saturday morning. Overtime was rarely paid, and she was expected to do overtime whenever it was required. This did not always give the young women time to take advantage of the new recreational activities which had been created in the twenties and thirties,. If she lived in the suburbs, she might not return home until 7 o'clock or even later in the evening. As one woman commented:

'We never got the bank holiday made up if you lost them in a holiday. The only thing was, if anyone had August bank holiday during their fortnight's holiday, then they had Saturday morning off, but otherwise you didn't get Saturday morning before a holiday, which I thought was rather mean really. I think looking at it now, that our supervisor could have done more, but I think she was scared of losing her job because the manager could be a bit spiteful. He would say, "Oh well, if you don't suit me there's plenty willing to take over your work." I don't think he would have done anything, but there was always that threat, you see.'

'What sort of things do you think she could have done?'

'I think she could have suggested that we had Saturday morning off for one thing for a holiday, and I know with this overtime I used to say to her we should have one evening a week, when whatever, if the work's piled to the ceiling, we can still go, so that if anyone wants to book a theatre or anything like that, well then they can go. Well she didn't do anything about that . . . but I think everyone was afraid of the boss and our supervisor was afraid of the manager. I suppose we were afraid of her in a way. I think that was really wrong.'

Although unemployment did not effect London as much as the regions with traditional industries, there was still an oversupply of trained clerks, which made competition fierce. Moreover, very few clerks had the backing of unions which, for a number of reasons, had developed slowly and sporadically and were usually only found in the Civil Service.

Female clerical workers were particularly noted for their lack of collective organisation and several theories have been formulated to explain this situation. These arguments are based on four assumptions. Firstly, a high proportion of women in an occupation has been a factor in lack of unionisation because women did not participate continuously in the labour market, because marriage or family responsibilities curtailed their employment. Secondly, women's pay was not the main source of income of the family and it was usually seen as supplementing the family wage. Thirdly, women entered secondary jobs where replacement was easy, making collective action ineffective. Fourthly, that middle-class values and an abhorrence of working-class tactics were a brake on the growth of unions.

Although clerical workers did pride themselves on their middle-class respectability, this is not an adequate explanation for the lack of unionisation. Lack of organisation was more an effect than a cause. It has been demonstrated, also, that a high proportion of women in clerical work is not the reason for lack of unionisation. In fact their participation in unions has been proportionate to their participation in the labour market.

What we are looking at broadly, are two types of female clerical workers, and unionisation was dependent, not so much on sex-composition or middle-class values, but the actual work setting and employment concentration. In the more bureaucratic organisations, such as the civil service after 1920, criteria for grading, qualification, remuneration and promotion were created. Employees were treated, not as individuals, but as members of groups. Identification was with the worker performing similar functions and an occupational consciousness was created. In the smaller offices in commercial and industrial establishments, conditions of work were not uniform. Women worked alongside members of different occupations and grades of work, jobs had their own particular characteristics, mobility and promotional opportunities did not follow any standard pattern and identification was not with the person carrying out similar functions. Unions were found in the former but were much weaker in the latter situation.

The women interviewed who worked in commercial and industrial offices often stated that they were unaware of the existence of clerical unions, and some felt that unionisation was not possible in the smaller establishments. Moreover, the conditions which prevailed in the 1920s and 1930s were not conducive for collective organisation:

'Did any member in the office belong to a trade union?'

'No. It was too small really. No, no. You see firms were small weren't they? You see, if you didn't like it they'd say go. But you couldn't go.'

'There were few clerical unions about at that time weren't there?'

'I don't know – not that I knew of. Very small I should think. And you see who is going to join? If you are one girl in a small firm you're not going to join, because if you say, "My union says come out," they'd say "Well go out." No, my boss wouldn't have liked that. He said, "I can look after my . . . my staff are my responsibility and I can look after them.'

*   *   *

The choosing of office work for a girl was based on the aspirations of the family and, to a certain extent, family income needs. It was also dependent on the position of the family cycle. For example, if the girl had older brothers and sisters who were either contributing to the family wage or had left home, she might have more opportunity to train as a shorthand typist, than a girl who was the eldest child in the family and whose wage was more essential.

Although a daughter's contribution varied during the period and was dependent on the economic position of the family, even when she could claim a larger share of her earnings, she was not necessarily mistress of her own life because she was an independent wage earner. Parental ties were extremely strong and ultimately determined her schooling, her work and life in general. Her attendance at grammar school, for example, would depend on family income, and on the value the parents placed on selective schooling.

During the interviewing of former shorthand typists, it was found that mothers were particularly influential in choosing the girls' occupations. This might have depended on the mothers' previous occupations or the area in which the family lived, and of course, the mother usually controlled the family budget. She often chose a job so that her daughter was working near a relative or she might have chosen a prestigious company, where there were opportunities for advancement. Interviews also revealed that other kinship ties were important. If the immediate family could not afford the fees for commercial education, relatives might pay the expenses. Thus the girl would have had further responsibilities, in terms of achievement, because she would have been scrutinised by relatives outside of the immediate family unit.

Parents and relatives played an important part in choosing the occupation, not least because at fourteen or fifteen most of the women interviewed indicated that they had little idea about employment. Many said that they did not think for themselves and let their parents tell them what to do, and, office work had been seen as the basis of raising the child's status. Parental influence was extremely strong throughout their working lives. Parents often chose the companies the women worked in, chose their friends and controlled their wage. In some cases the whole wage was given, usually to the mother, who would give the girl back a certain amount for clothing, fares, lunches and entertainment. It was often a sign of maturity when the girl was able to keep some of her wage in order to buy her own clothes. The wage allocation differed according to the need of the family. In some cases only a small part of the wage was given to the mother, and one woman who came from a middle-class background gave a certain amount to her mother each week who put it away into a savings account. She was also supplemented by her father, who brought her clothes and paid for her lunches and holidays.

However, social and economic circumstances had changed so that middle-class parents could no longer scrutinise the men their daughters were mixing with in the office and a minority of daughters often lived away from homes in hostels or clubs in central London. Nevertheless, life for the middle- and lower-middle-class woman living in London was not as emancipating as was often suggested. Expenditure had to be carefully allocated, and strict discipline was enforced in the hostels. One woman interviewed, described the hostel she lived in during the late 1930s:

'I was living in a hostel in Vauxhall Bridge Road which was run for single business ladies, and some of whom were extremely antique by my standards. But they were the smallest rooms I've ever inhabited, they were really partitioned. I mean they were rooms, but they were so narrow, there was just room for a bed and a little tiny sort of gangway and a chest of drawers. They were very small. And, we had a washbasin. But then they didn't charge much. I mean you were right in the middle of London and you had breakfast everyday and all meals at the weekend if you stayed there – only I always went home – and your laundry, that is to say, your sheets and pillow cases, for 30s a week. That was half my wages, but still, you got everything really.'

Most women were glad to have a job and expectations went little further than some leisure activities before marriage. Office romances between bosses and secretaries might have existed, but were usually a fantasy of Hollywood or the weekly magazines. On the whole, women in offices had responsibilities to their families, and any show of independence was brief, before they entered married life. Their contribution to the home might also entail some household chores such as ironing or sewing during the evening.

Perhaps some of the anxieties expressed stemmed more from the fear that women would not want to leave the labour market to enter the confines of domesticity. However, the economic, demographic and ideological conditions after the First World War meant that women had little alternative than to leave the labour market. Moreover, mixing with peers, both in the office and in outside activities promoted by their work, meant that women had greater opportunities of meeting future husbands rather than the deferment of marriage. Given the unequal opportunities women had in the labour market and the importance placed on child-care and housekeeping, most women looked forward to leaving work and marriage was seen as 'freedom' as opposed to the more restricting nature of the workplace. This was a strong reason why women did not challenge the existing sexual divisions in the labour market:

'So the company had a rule that they didn't employ married women?'

'Yes, it was a sort of unwritten rule, I think. You reckoned to leave. Mind you, you were jolly glad to leave. I was . . . I liked the freedom of being at home and looking after a home. Still think it's best, but there you are.'

Companies generally adhered to the prevailing norms and throughout the period, most offices had a rule not to employ married women, the Civil Service being especially strict in the enforcement of this rule. Some offices would employ a married woman if her husband was ill or unemployed, or sometimes, if the boss did not want to lose the services of his secretary. This latter case was extremely rare, and employment would be terminated if the woman was pregnant.

A woman who sought outside employment might also have to assume a single identity. There was not only the social stigma of working whilst married, but also the accusation of taking a single woman's job:

'Most girls would leave an office on marriage but conditions in my home were such that I felt my mother should not be left without some continuing help . . . I had a very hard time from some of the other girls who were resentful that I "was taking a single girl's place", and I tried hard to find other employment which took until 1929. To do this I took off my wedding ring and called myself "Miss Adams".'

One woman interviewed, who worked as a secretary in local government, said she was resolved not to marry because women in the 1920s and 1930s were unable to combine work and marriage:

'Why didn't you want to marry?'

'Oh, I don't know – I always said I wouldn't marry. And when I tell you that when I married I was 61 you'll see that I kept it up. I didn't marry until after I had retired. I don't regret it, we had eight very happy years. I wasn't interested in marriage, as such, I always wanted a career and I had one.'

'Do you think many women thought like that?'

'No. I think I was an exception. I mean it wasn't that I didn't like men – I enjoyed their company. I used to go to dances – we used to have a lot of tennis dances, they were great fun. But I didn't feel that I wanted to settle down into the routine. And, of course, in those days, you didn't really think of marriage and a job. It was exceptional. For instance, in local government you weren't allowed to keep a job if you married and teachers weren't allowed to keep their jobs if they married. So it was a question really of one or the other. That was how it happened.'

For some, there might have been some initial reluctance to leave their work, but, on the whole, women accepted their domestic role and employment was only sought in times of economic hardship. Women would sometimes work in outside employment or, because of their experience, they might help their husbands if they were self-employed and had businesses of their own.

Office work, therefore, did very little for women's emancipation. In fact, there was no overall increase in real terms of women's employment. Rather, there was a redistribution of women working in domestic production and service to the clerical sector, the numbers being increasingly represented by single women. Moreover, the work of the secretary and shorthand-typist reinforced traditional female characteristics:

> The secretary has often been termed an 'office-wife' and indeed there are similarities between them where the wife is also a housewife. They are both not only supportive towards, but dependent upon a particular individual for income and status, and for many secretaries the work role is seen as the creation of a relationship, just as a marriage is between husbands and wives.[6]

Although job functions were standardised in the Civil Service, the majority of shorthand typists' work was based on the personal relationship between herself and her boss and was effectively away from organisational scrutiny. In this private setting, few shorthand typists acquired an occupational consciousness and their allegiance was most definitely with their boss or company rather than other shorthand typists. Female clerical workers did not have loyalties to clerical workers as a group. Their participation in union organisation was determined by the setting and functions of their work.

Although the class composition of the occupation was gradually changing and more women with working-class origins were entering, the occupation still retained status and respectability in comparison to manual occupations. The workforce had both grammar and elementary education, and many added commercial training. Furthermore, the working relationship retained an aura of respectability, a characteristic which had existed in the counting house period, and which, despite important structural changes in clerical work, had not been completely eroded.

Women in offices had different experiences and attitudes to work, depending on what part of the period they worked. It is probable that workers in the first 20 years of the century placed a higher importance on work. They were likely to spend at least ten years in an office even if they married, and considerably longer if they remained single. This was a period of much debate about the occupation as a 'profession'. Although standards were not eroded in the 1920s and 1930s and it was important to have a job, female office workers generally spent less time at work and their priorities were more than ever governed by their future domestic role.

Notes

1. Gregory Anderson, *Victorian Clerks*, 1976, p. 102.
2. *Pitman's Metropolitan School of Shorthand*, 1893, p. 17.
3. Lee Holcombe, *Victorian Ladies at Work*, 1973, p. 175.
4. David Lockwood, *The Blackcoated Worker*, 1958, p. 106.
5. Holcombe, p. 176.
6. Rosalie Silverstone, *How the Law put an End to the Dolly Bird Ads*, 1978, p. 27.

7 'A Pension to Look Forward to . . .?': Women Civil Service Clerks in London, 1925–1939

KAY SANDERSON

The ten women[1] whose life histories form the basis of this study were, for part of their lives, clerical grade civil servants. They were all born between 1905 and 1915 and had a Civil Service career of at least seven years. These women were able to achieve *for themselves* upward social mobility into the (lower) middle class; this change in their social position happening before and not as a result of, marriage to similarly upwardly mobile men. This intra-generational change can only be understood by placing the individual life histories within a social and economic context. As C. W. Mills pointed out more than 25 years ago '. . . every individual lives from one generation to the next, in some society; he lives out a biography and he lives it out within some historical sequence.'[2] One supposes that the same goes for 'she' too. This self evident truth about individual life experience is, surprisingly, almost ignored in classic studies of social mobility.

The families of the women in the study were rather similar, they were mostly, the daughters of small business or artisan fathers. One father died young, of the others 5 were self employed (2 plumbers, 2 small shopkeepers, 1 decorator) 2 were engineers, one of whom worked for the Gas Board and one mostly in India. All the fathers were elementary school educated and had left school by the age 13–14 years. The mothers had the same educational background and they had all worked in the female 'personal service' sector: 6 had been in domestic service, 2 were seamstresses and one, unusually, had been a clerk. All the families were relatively hard up and all but one had experienced periods of unemployment for the father, however only the widowed mother was in waged work after

145

marriage (she was a live-in caretaker/cleaner). The families were all very 'respectable' and even the poorest family 'kept up standards':

> 'They were very poor streets [where I lived] the houses backed onto the road, well anyway, they were all respectable families, not slums really, not like some places in London now – dirty. They weren't dirty, you know, you'd have hearthstoned front doorsteps, lace curtains at the windows, even though the houses faced bang onto the pavement.'

This family was the largest, with four children, all the others had only one or two children. There is no doubt that this factor in their childhood was very significant; the investment of family resources and ambition being focused rather than divided between many children.

Before looking in some detail into the working life of the women – the career phase that occurred before marriage – it is worthwhile to place this part of their life cycle in a more extended context. From the age of eleven onwards their biographies began to diverge from that of their parents (especially their mothers) and it was education that first moved the women onto a different track. Their parents were educated during the last years of the nineteenth century, at which time an elementary education (to age 12 or thereabouts) was the normal experience of all children outside the wealthy middle and upper classes. The advantaged minority were able to continue their education at a secondary level in Public Schools and in 'old foundation' Grammar schools. It was these schools that provided the classics-based education that was considered appropriate to the future members of the ruling and professional classes. For the rest, elementary schools provided structured and disciplined schooling at a basic level. This spartan training in the '3Rs' was the experience of the majority of British children throughout the inter-war period.

However, from the end of the First World War onwards, the idea that bright children should be able to continue their education at a secondary level, regardless of their ability to pay, began to gain ground. In fact the number of elementary school children who were able to transfer to secondary school remained small. As late as 1928 only 8 per cent of these children were selected for further education. Nevertheless, these post-war children were, effectively, the first generation of children from poorer families with any chance to enter the middle-class educational system. The women clerks in this study were part of this privileged minority.

This 8 per cent of children were selected from the elementary schools by a competitive examination taken at eleven and the successful candidates were given 'scholarships' (subsidised places) in local secondary schools, the places being paid for by the local Education Authorities; (the majority of secondary school pupils were fee paying, 75 per cent in 1920, declining to 50 per cent in 1932). The women in the study were very aware of their privileged position, a position they had, nevertheless, earned for themselves by their diligence and efforts at elementary school. By passing the exam and taking a place at secondary school they began to distance themselves from their elementary school peers and from other members of their family – they did not, however, become an indistinguishable part of the middle-class system they had entered:

'They [the education authority] gave you a list of all the schools in the area, you could have applied to any of them, we chose a girls' secondary school nearby . . . well, you see, there were three grades A, B and C, and all the A grade were scholarship girls and the B and C paid, so we were a minority. We had diplomats' daughters there, people like that . . . we were the brains of the school, but of course, we didn't have the same clothes as they did, no money or anything like that, but I was grateful, if you can understand, I was grateful for the opportunity, though I never felt I was on their level . . . though I did go to their school.'

'I was the first child from that elementary school to get a scholarship to "Howells" which was really a school for the daughters of gentlefolk, whereas the scholarship girls were expected to get the results.'

Many of the scholarship children went to County secondary schools, established after the First World War by the local authorities on the grammar school model; these did not have such a 'daughters of gentlefolk' tradition but did, like the grammar schools, provide a rigorous education, to boys and girls alike, in sciences, arts and languages, leading to a comprehensive examination, the Matriculation, after five years. It was the scholarship children who were expected to, and did, shine in these public examinations.

The schooling and education available during this period has been described in some detail because it was so significant in the lives and attitudes of these clever non-middle-class girls. At eleven, they found themselves, in all-girl schools, with good equipment, in small classes, taught by well-educated, highly motivated women (first and second generation feminists and products of the First World War) and studying 'difficult' subjects such as physics, chemistry and languages: in short, enjoying the sort of education that had been developed for middle class boys.

'I thought it was a privilege to go there, I worked hard, especially for 'matric' I gave up all my holidays for studying . . . I did chemistry and physics, the top ones did that, the others [fee paying girls] did botany; we had a very good chemistry teacher, that was the subject I loved best, and the physics teacher – she was very well educated. We had this maths teacher, she had been brought up in a boys' school, and she had that masculine approach, I think that was why she was good at maths . . . and we did french and latin, oh yes, and music; and a marvellous gym, we did hockey and netball; we had separate labs for physics and chemistry and there was a school library, oh yes, it really was a good school.

Unlike a later generation of women – their daughters for example – who thought it amusing of 'feminine' to be 'hopeless at sciences and maths', these girls' status in their schools depended on their ability to do well at difficult (boys') subjects. Most importantly, their time at secondary school established for them a contradictory and complicated social position – and one that they only shared with other 'selected' clever but poorer children – and this was to become a feature of their adult life.

The standing of these girls with their elementary educated parents and peers was very high, they had conspicuously 'done well'; but their position in the middle-class institution was specifically tied to their conformity and diligence – their ability to pass exams. Originality and ambition were not encouraged. Unlike middle class boys, these girls were not 'educated for leadership', nor were they able to remain at school after matriculation to take the advanced level exams[3] at 17–18 years old (these examinations being the prerequisite to university entrance). Neither the finances nor the expectations of the girls and their parents extended beyond the Matriculation. They had got onto the educational ladder, that was achievement enough, they did not aspire to rise much beyond the bottom rungs.

The women, leaving school after the Matriculation, were already two years 'behind' their elementary school peers who had left school, and started work at 14. For the working-class family at that time the loss of a wage earner for two years was a significant sacrifice for the family. Not surprisingly, these daughters felt an obligation to repay this investment by finding a well paid and secure job as soon as possible. The relatively well paid jobs for which they were now qualified were, of course, in the white-collar secretarial and clerical sector. Within this sector the Civil Service offered the best prospects; the salary level was comparable to, or better than, the private sector, and there were all the fringe benefits of a 'career' – an incremental salary scale, pension scheme, health care and real job security. It must be remembered that this period, (approximately 1925–35) when the women were making decisions about their careers, was very insecure for skilled manual workers and skilled artisans; all their fathers belonged in this category and all but one experienced some unemployment during the 1920–39 period. It is not surprising that the girls found themselves under pressure, especially from their fathers, to compete for one of the desirable Civil Service positions.

> 'In those days, funnily enough, you did what you were told, you really did what father said . . . I think [that what he wanted] was security as regards a job, he didn't want that we would be in and out of different jobs, he wanted us to have a pension to look forward to.'

They did express some regret that they couldn't pursue more interesting careers, and none of the women remembers feeling any great enthusiasm for the job itself, even though they appreciated the material advantages.

> 'I did know a couple [of fellow students] who eventually went to university, but that was very difficult for us because there were no grants as such . . . what I really wanted was to be an analytical

chemist, but to do that you had to take a job at a very low salary and study in your spare time, and I thought it was about time I earned some money, so I entered the Civil Service Exam . . .'

'I could have gone on to take 'Higher Schools', but I had to leave at 17, I had to go to work then . . . my art teacher sent me all my drawings that I'd left behind at school and I had a lovely letter and she said in it "you should do portrait painting" [laugh]. Well, that was an impossibility for me . . . [about the Civil Service Exam] . . . it was just 'the thing' to take it, and I hated maths, yet I got a job that was all maths.'

The way into the Civil Service, as suggested, was via a very competitive examination. Once again the women were attempting to enter a traditional middle-class institution by demonstrating their ability to pass examinations. However, their entry into the job market was not entirely a replay of their entry into secondary school; this time their *gender* as well as their class background, was a critical aspect of their recruitment and career development. Women's position in the Civil Service mirrored their position in the overall occupational structure – they filled the routine semi-skilled and unskilled positions at the bottom of the hierarchy. However, before discussing their experiences as 'women servants of the state', their individual biographies can, again, usefully be placed in a wider context.

The inter-war period saw demographic changes as well as changes in the occupational structure and these affected and reflected, their experiences as young unmarried working women. First, they entered the labour market at a time when the percentage of never-married women in the population was unusually high (due to the male fatalities of the First World War) and the percentage of single women engaged in economic activity was increasing (although it was not until after the Second World War that married women became a significant part of the labour force). Secondly, the occupational structure itself was changing shape. The main feature of the inter-war period was the great increase in lower-level white collar work and the parallel decline in semi-skilled and skilled manual work. It was (single) women who were recruited to the clerical jobs in the expanding financial, business and government bureaucracies.

Within the Civil Service women were a minority of employees, about 25 per cent of the total establishment, throughout the period; they were recruited to all-female grades to do routine clerical work. The turnover of women was high since the Civil Service operated a formal marriage bar until the Second World War which obliged all women (but no men) to resign on marriage. Since most women did marry, the marriage bar ensured short female careers and some advantage to the State.[4] Whereas male Civil Servants could look forward to careers lasting more than 40 years, and to moving, albeit slowly, up through the bureaucratic hierarchy, women would not expect to remain for more than 10 years at most. This ban effectively, and psychologically, stalled the careers of the women; their employment was 'temporary' and 'short term', not something to be taken very seriously. They could only make a personal commitment to a Civil Service career at the cost of abandoning expectations and hopes of marriage. Even for the potentially ambitious women the career ladder was blocked – by single women born 10–20 years earlier. These were the 'unclaimed treasures' whose potential husbands had been killed during the 1914–18 war. The women of the 1905 to 1915 generation entered, by a competitive examination, into all-female dead-end niches within the service where their diligence and docility, but not their intelligence, were their major assets. The regulations ensured that they left before they became too discontented, ambitious or expensive.

The major employing department in the Civil Service was the Post Office – taking 68 per cent of the women and 59 per cent of the men. Women were employed as Post Office clerks, as telephonists and in the Post Office Savings Bank.

'The first thing you saw when you went in was this big tied up bundle of postal orders, and *that* was your day's work, you had to do that before you left and went home. Well you had a big board with slots in, you see, and you sat and sorted all the postal orders into numbers, coding numbers, then you went into another room where you pulled out slots and packed them in, they were sorted into numerical order again . . . sometimes you had an awful job to fit one in, but you *had* to finish all that work in one day, you couldn't leave it until the next day . . . it was an awful lot of pressure to get it done, but you see, you didn't think that, you just accepted that was your day's work.'

'It was a big place [the Post Office Savings Bank], well it had 3000 people there, it was the Headquarters you see, it was on four floors with big windows, bright offices; you could just see the end of the room from the other, a huge place. Of course, in those days every error you made counted against you – they couldn't do it now – and also you were on a year's probation and could be turfed out after a year; so it was quite disciplined, but you see it was the depression and you hung onto your jobs. . . .'

Nor did the women recruited into other departments have more challenging jobs: two of the women recall doing simple accounts seated at a moving table – a conveyor belt bringing their work to them. As older women they are somewhat puzzled at their extreme docility in their youth; they take pride in the fact they 'put up with it', in their endurance; but they cannot recall why they didn't feel more resentment at the mindless tasks they were set to do. They were, and knew they were, conspicuously over-qualified for the work they were doing. The 'rational management' and division of labour experienced by assembly-line manual workers was the model for these routine office workers. However, their *prestige* as white-collar Civil Servants was not much affected by the *reality* of their work:

'The other girls in the street thought I was a bit toffee nosed, some of them worked at Glaxo or Lyons, in the offices or even in the works itself . . . there were a lot of places for girls, but not Civil Service type of job . . .'

and of course, their fellow workers were also 'well-educated' girls.

'It wasn't a bit like today, not at all – I mean, I know that appearances are deceptive, but, well everybody seemed the same in those days, we were mostly secondary school girls, we all took great care with our appearances, we all dressed nicely.'

All of the women formed close friendships with the 'girls from the office'; many of these friendships still continuing 50 years later. They progressively spent more of their non-working hours with these office friends, going to the theatre, concerts, cinema, playing tennis and going on other outings, at the same time becoming less attached to the family circle. Nevertheless, it did not occur to any of them to leave home, nor could they recall anybody who had done so. They all felt that they had a responsibility to contribute to the family income, sharing, with their fathers, the position of bread-winners. In return they, like him, enjoyed the domestic services of their mothers. Mother also controlled the family budgeting in all these households, the breadwinners handing over their wages for her to manage.

'Mother just continued doing all the domestic sort of thing, although I did contribute to the family purse. I just didn't learn anything about domestic work . . .'

'I don't know why we did really [live at home], it was the discipline – the ties there, you accepted it. My mother sort of, well, we gave her our wages and got back pocket money. I think that her great mistake was not to let us have control of our own money, perhaps that wasn't exactly the right thing to do. . . .'

'Well, the girls I mixed with gave a fair amount, most of them, most of the girls I knew . . . they thought it their duty, really, to give it to their mums.'

During their 1920s, the women began to distance themselves from the domestic life style of their parents. In all the cases, as suggested, the families operated on the basis of very segregated roles within the marriage, and this became a model for everything they did not want in their own future married role. At the same time none of them doubted that their future domestic life would involve being a full time housewife, but they wanted an equal partnership. They had come to dislike the idea and the reality of a traditional household with an authoritarian male head. As young working women in well paid and prestigious employment they had a high standing in the family and were not so inclined to defer to 'father'. One of them describes how she came to a more equal relationship with her father:

'We used to talk a lot in our family, as I got older, you know, and he did listen a bit . . . but he never regarded her [mother] as his equal – ever – she was just his wife, it was the Victorian idea which I didn't like, I held it against my father that; I saw it at the time, he used to say there were too many women in the house [laugh] well there were really when you came to work it out [there were two daughters and no son] and we started to get a bit "women's lib" style. Well I did, I used to say "don't talk to Mum like that" . . . I've always had thoughts like that, you know, opinions. I suppose that's why I didn't get married till I was 26 [laugh] because I wanted someone who would treat me as an equal.'

In fact this woman was the youngest bride; the mean age for the group being 29. As they moved into their mid-twenties they did begin to put their minds more seriously to finding a suitable husband and setting up a home of their own. What they were looking for, as suggested above, was a man whom they could enjoy an equal relationship:

'Somebody like oneself, the same educational background, say local government of the Civil Service, someone steady with a similar attitude and outlook . . .'

'I think you went out with men of your own class, more or less, yes, say office people; one I used to know worked for a solicitor, another was an optician, you see? Yes, and there were people from the Post Office, and my friend's brother, he was a jeweller in Regent Street – they had good positions. We all had nice, what I call nice, friends; they were decent people with decent manners and dressing, men with good steady jobs, with nice habits, clean hands – you see? [laugh].'

Having found a suitable young man they did not rush into marriage. First they saved up for their new home. All of them had experienced some poverty in their childhoods, of their mothers having to 'make do and mend', this was not how they wished to start their new 'career' as housewives:

'Now there was a funny thing that happened then, we used to become engaged, then we'd save terribly hard for three or four years, which you wouldn't dream of doing now; we all saved hard to have nice homes to start off with – we all had a bottom drawer it was called. It was such a thrill too I can tell you [laugh] and the dowry was a great help too, mine was £169 if I remember.'

'Once you were engaged, which gave you 2 years, you bought all your linen and bedding and curtains, my husband helped with those . . . and we made all our satin underwear, french knickers, petticoats and nightgowns – We all had our own furniture, we bought it with the dowry – I had about £100 . . .'

The 'dowry' which they all mentioned, remembering the exact amount, was actually a gratuity in lieu of pension. It was paid to women when they resigned to get married, thus making them a rather good 'catch' for an aspiring man. The gratuity was paid at the rate of one month's pay for each year of service, but not exceeding twelve months pay. It was not financially worthwhile for a woman to stay in the service beyond 12 years, as the gratuity would cease to accumulate after this. After 12 years a woman would only get a proper return on her pension contributions if she stayed in the Service to retirement, and stayed *single*. The 12-year limit on the 'dowry' was thus another subtle pressure on female civil servants to have short careers, to leave before they became too expensive to the state.

In any case, by their mid to late twenties the women had acquired three strong aspirations – to leave the daily grind of the Civil Service, to leave the natal home for the 'independence' of a home of their own, and, above all, to avoid the fate of the single 'unclaimed treasures' who were blocking the promotion ladder ahead of them, and who were, at 50 or even 60, still living at home.

'Given the choice we would rather have a short career then get married, but short of that they [sic] would settle for a long career in a secure job – what I wanted, more than anything, was to get married and have my own home.'

None of the women doubted that marriage and domestic life was the most desirable step they could take, nor did they, initially at least, have any doubts about reaching the end of the 'career' phase of their life.

'Usually you'd try, after you were married, to have some of your office friends down, to show off really, wasn't it? Your nice new home and all the nice things in it, you know [laugh], they'd think how lucky you were: "Hasn't she done well for herself". I did have a nice home as a matter of fact, all absolutely spot new . . .'

'All the girls from the office thought I'd got a smashing home, lovely, I was full of it. We had everything mind you, we saved up to buy everything new . . .'

They had not, it is true, acquired this new and happy position by passing an exam, but they had earned their 'lovely new homes' by their own hard work and sensible management. Their new status, as fully set up middle class housewives, was no more an ascribed status than their school and career positions had been. They were, with men of 'a similar background to oneself', engaged in the establishment of a new partnership-based life style, a life style suited to a well educated ex-civil servant.

As suggested, the women entered domestic life with enthusiasm. They saw themselves as finally arrived at their proper and most fulfilling stage in life. Marriage had rescued them from the pressures of tedious and taxing clerical work and from a domestic life at home over which they had little or no control. No wonder they, paradoxically, saw the move to financially dependent house-keeping as a significant move towards independence.

'We [married ones] never wanted to go back and do what they were doing at the office; we wouldn't have swapped with them [laugh]. To own your own home was a kind of *status* you see . . ., on marriage you changed, you changed your status and changed your life completely.'

This feeling of independence was sustained by the 'different but equal' relationships they set up with their husbands.

'What my husband and I did, we sorted everything out ourselves. He earned £3 a week which wasn't bad for those days and on Tuesday nights [the day before he was paid] we'd put on the table what we'd got between us, according to what was needed we'd split it.'

'Yes, I had 27s 6d a week for food, coal, newspapers, he paid the rent and we put so much aside for holidays and things like that.

We always knew what the other was doing, that's the point, we shared everything.'

'It might seem awfully trite, but Jim and I were awfully close knit, we sort of didn't have any problems. We had a very happy – a very peaceful married life you know, we sorted things out ourselves. That's why it was such a . . . miss . . . when he went, because I didn't have anybody, really to . . . he was that type of person, he always had time to listen to his children and time to listen to me, he was a very nice man . . .'

The work of a housewife was seen as a responsible *job* and one in which, for the first time, the women were able to exercise some autonomy and control. *The Marriage Book* (published about 1935), as well as being an extensive manual of housekeeping practice also summed up the prevailing ideology of middle class housewifery.

She [a woman] is handicapped unless she really knows how to keep house. This does not mean a return to domestic slavery, but the emancipation of taking a lively interest in the things she ought to know. On no account should good housekeeping be presented as drudgery, but as a real and exciting achievement . . . House pride goes naturally with good housekeeping. The woman who possesses it in full measure takes a personal joy in cleaning and polishing, in making her glass sparkle and her silver shine. There is, again, a great feeling for beauty, and an orderly, well arranged, home is one of its best expressions.[5]

One of the women explained what she meant when she described a woman as a 'good wife and mother':

'Well, getting three meals a day, keeping the house clean, doing the cooking, baking and mending and washing and looking after the children properly, bringing them up properly, well behaved, well trained children . . . that wouldn't disgrace you . . . Getting married was taking on a job – it was up to you to do the job to the best of your ability, in return you got a nice home and what you needed . . . so all these tasks [housework] had to have priority.'

The outbreak of war in 1939, temporarily, turned these women's attention away from responsibilities of domestic life. Three of the married (but childless) women were called up and returned to the Civil Service. Unlike the women who were still single at the outbreak of war, the married women were allocated routine low-skill tasks of similar or lower level than they had achieved during their earlier career. For them the war did not have a radical effect on their lives, but was, rather, 'an experience' to be endured until they were able to return to domestic life.

> 'Of course during the war if you hadn't got a family they expected you to go back to work . . . it was an experience, everyday you had to put on your gas mask and helmet for half an hour. Also we had to do night duty, you slept downstairs . . . It was just for a while, as soon as you were released you went back to being a housewife.'

For those who were still single the war did open up many opportunities for career advancement, two reaching the high level of Executive Grade.

> 'Normally to become an Executive Officer you had to have been to University – there was an exam, but really and truly you needed the University education; but during the war, when all the men had gone you see, you could get it by promotion. And I got it by promotion.'

> 'When my first promotion came it was great joy – it all suddenly became much more interesting . . . it was particularly challenging, you see, you were dealing with items in short supply and there was a lot of difficulties. But you just worked it out in your own way – this was rather fun actually.'

The others, too, found themselves in different and more interesting niches within the Civil Service.

The wartime careers will not be discussed in detail, but two points are worth making about these older career 'girls'. Those who had responsible and/or high level jobs were not willing to be 'dogsbody clerks' again, and at least three of the women had become the most significant breadwinner in the natal family, and were beginning to feel the weight of 'obligation' to remain at home permanently. Not surprisingly, all, except one, chose marriage as a solution to the problem of approaching maiden aunthood.

The husbands of the women in the study were, more or less, what the women had been looking for. All had been to Grammar School, 7 were in public service (4 Civil Servants, an education officer, a railway clerk and a CID officer), one was an optician and one worked at the Stock Exchange. Between them the women had 15 children (3 had none); of these children, born between 1940–1953, 13 passed the 11+ examination to Grammar School and 7 continued to university (which none of their parents had done).

The social mobility achieved by these women Civil Servants within their own life cycle can thus be seen as an intermediate stage. They were the bridge between their elementary school educated, skilled working-class parents and their securely middle-class children. As this partial discussion of their lives suggests, it was the unique combination of social historical context, combined with their class and gender specific characteristics of docility and deference, that facilitated their movement from the traditional artisan working class to the white-collar lower middle-class. Their successful crossing of this bridge was a result of these women's ability to use new educational and employment opportunities to achieve a position which was later confirmed by marriage to men who had taken a similar route.

Notes

1. These women were part of a larger group of clerical workers of the same age cohort whose life histories were collected as part of an intensive case study of social mobility.
2. C. Wright Mills, *The Sociological Imagination*, 1959, p. 6.
3. There is a gender difference at this level as well as a class one. Girls were less likely than boys to take the Higher Matriculation courses, they were particularly badly represented in the sciences and classics (Latin and Greek); the girls who were able to stay on at school opted instead for arts subjects – languages and literature.
   Figures for 1928 from the *Board of Education Report*, 1927–28 showing Advanced level courses available:

Subject	Boys Schools	Girls Schools	Co-Ed Schools
Sciences	143	30	34
Classics	34	2	—
Modern	57	99	24
Total	234	131	58

4. The view of the *Tomlin Commission of the Civil Service* 1929–31 was: 'The view held by the majority may be stated as follows: (1) The main argument against the retention of the marriage bar is that it may result in the loss to the service of experienced workers. This argument no doubt has weight as regards officers in the higher grades. On the other hand, in regard to certain classes such as writing assistants (clerks) class, retirement on marriage results in securing a rapid turnover of staff employed on routine duties. This is an advantage. In this connection figures supplied to us by the Government Actuary, based on Post Office experience, showing that of 10 000 women in the service at the age of 20, 2207 leave on account of marriage before reaching the age of 25, and a further 2777 before reaching the age of 30.'

5. *The Marriage Book*, The Amalgamated Press Ltd, London, C. 1935, p. 328.

8 'The Girl Behind the Man Behind the Gun': The Women's Army Auxiliary Corps, 1914–18

ELIZABETH CROSTHWAIT

When the idea of a women's corps attached to the armed services was first raised, it received the same kind of ridicule and disbelief which had earlier surrounded proposals for women police and for many of the same reasons. Women in the army seemed to be the opposite of Victorian feminity that was based on family-centred dependence and weakness. A soldier had to be aggressive, independent of emotional ties with allegiance only to his superiors. Yet by the end of the war in 1918, a Women's Auxiliary was established as part of the British Army. The way this change came about, the problems and tensions it created for the men of the army, the general public and particularly for the women volunteers themselves are the focus of this chapter.

The shift to a war economy had inflamed existing underemployment and by 1914, many of those working in traditional women's trades were losing their jobs. A Central Committee on Women's Employment was set up with Mary MacArthur, of the National Federation of Women Workers, as its secretary. Its main function was to draw up various schemes for the employment of women. By March 1915, responding to the demands of war, the government had compiled a register of women willing to do industrial, agricultural or clerical work. This exercise itself alerted people to the pool of woman power available to the nation. The realisation that women could, in fact, do jobs long believed beyond their powers came in the summer and autumn of 1915 and was as much a result of economic necessity than direct feminist pressure.[1] Two crucial factors transformed opportunities for women's work: the shortage of munitions and the shortage of soldiers which led to universal male conscription in May 1916. The 500 000 women working in commerce in 1914 doubled by 1918 as did the 200 000 in national and local government employment, mainly clerical workers. Other, mainly middle and upper-class women, volunteered as nursing aides or for the Women's Land Army.

For working class women, wider opportunities opened in occupations traditionally designated as masculine. Transport experienced the biggest increase of women workers, growing sevenfold to 117 000. The most dramatic change, however, came in munitions production. By 1918, there were nearly a million women employed in munitions factories, many of them former domestic servants. Although relatively well paid in female terms, this was arduous work with long hours. It was also dangerous with frequent explosions; TNT poisoning caused the skin to turn yellow and earned munitions workers the nickname of 'canary girls'!

As the war progressed, women and girls were positively encouraged to leave home and go into industry, although many of them were overworked and underpaid. There was still general prejudice against the employment of women and continuing opposition to splitting up a man's job among several women (called *dilution*) which was the common practice when females were introduced into a traditionally male domain. The National Federation of Women Workers agreed to withdraw its members at the end of the war from those occupations claimed as men's by the Association of Skilled Engineers in return for acting jointly in wage negotiations for the duration.

With mounting casualties it was not only the engineering industry that felt the loss of manpower. The army itself consumed a never-ending stream of recruits and conscripts. Attention began to turn to the only untapped source of replacements: women. Undoubtedly, too, the agitation of feminists through the previous decades and their success in producing better educated, more ambitious young women had laid the groundwork for those who took the unusual step of volunteering for the untried path of Army life.

*   *   *

In March 1917 notices first appeared in the newspapers urging women to don khaki uniforms and join the newly formed Women's Army Auxiliary Corps. The decision to form such a corps was one of the most novel and problematic aspects of women's war work. The army had always been an exclusively male institution. All men, by virtue of their masculinity, could be included and share with other men the monopoly of legalised violence, the power and prestige vested in military activities. One of the themes of this chapter is to look at the contradictions of women's presence in this masculine organisation. Women in the army ran the risk of making it less important, and 'emasculating' (sic) the roles of soldiers.

Conversely, public fears were expressed about the effect of the army on women's femininity. The home, female delicateness and sensibility were threatened by the spectre of mannish, independent soldier women. And persistent fears about immorality were raised if women played an active role in this male dominated institution, inevitably being thrown into such close proximity to men. Women were suspected of both adopting masculine attributes and being rampantly sexual.

The army's need for womanpower was not sufficient reason to calm these fears and justify the women's presence. Apologies for the WAAC tried to counteract this disquiet and make it acceptable by locating the Corps within the context of the ideology of the home. Relationships between the women and the men, female officers and their charges were described as familial, the women's conditions as homely, and it was stressed that they serviced rather than served in the army.

Attention was also drawn to the benefits of army life for eugenic concerns about the nation's health. The WAAC could bestow physical health, self-discipline, and encourage personal cleanliness, all of which would improve women's abilities to be good wives and mothers. There was a contradiction between the fears about WAAC immorality and the images the propaganda presented to try and counteract them. The former reflected the old female stereotype of the sexual temptress, the latter that of the loving, caring, 'ministering angel'. It is relatively easy to trace these attitudes towards the corps and the women in it, at least from official sources although there is less material from serving soldiers. However it proved much more difficult to find out how women themselves perceived their position in the WAAC so that here oral history interviews have been especially useful.

Demands from middle and upper-class women to have control over the scheme were related to the pre-war struggle for the vote, and the 'equal rights' tradition of feminism inherent in that struggle. These women had demanded the vote not o upset social and political institutions but to be included in them. They wanted equal opportunity to serve the war effort, and the WAAC became a focus for this demand. However this also brought women into conflict with the War Office, which was determined to delegate as little authority and status as possible to them.

A very precise definition of the object of the WAAC was given in the Army Council Instruction No. 1069 of 7 July 1917, the formal basis of the scheme. It was to effect substitution of women for soldiers in certain areas of employments at home, and at the bases on the lines of communication overseas. Considerable stress was given to the point that no woman was to be employed unless a soldier was released for other purposes. This was a clear statement of the secondary role of the WAAC. There was no question of it being desirable in itself to have women in the army; the only justification could be in terms of the needs of men. The women could release men for the far more important task of fighting.

The Army's overriding concern about its strength in the field meant that its most valuable personnel were its fighting men. A much lower value was put on womanpower. They were non-combatants and were engaged in unskilled or semi-skilled routine work, so were easy to replace. If a woman became a problem – because of pregnancy, VD or indiscipline – she was discharged. The Army did not want the bother of giving her medical treatment or overseeing punishment. Members of the WAAC were not allowed to serve in the same theatre of war as their husbands. This was considered to be detrimental to efficiency and discipline, as husband and wife would be constantly trying to see each other instead of getting on with the job of fighting the war. In these cases it was obviously the woman who was dispensable. If a woman's husband was ordered to the same theatre of war, or if she married while abroad, then she was withdrawn and employed on Home Service. Unlike the soldiers who were expected to leave their private lives behind and owe their first loyalty to the Army, women's first duty was always to her family. Her family ties overrode the Army's claim on her services; marriage, illness of children, a husband's illness or discharge from the services necessitating the return of the wife to look after the home, or illness of a parent necessitating the presence of the woman permanently at home, were all considered compassionate grounds for discharge.

The presence of women in the Army required the military authorities to take on the unfamiliar role of moral guardians. Previously their dealings with sexuality had been confined to measures designed to check the spread of VD amongst the soldiers. For the WAACS, it was generally agreed that moral welfare was most properly the sphere of female officers. Indeed any suggestion that men had any direct dealings with the women when they were off duty provoked an outcry. One Area Controller in France was dismissed because she made an injudicious speech saying that the WAAC was so military that the male Base Commandant at Boulagne had the power to enter any girl's room at any hour of the day or night. This speech was taken down in shorthand and caused a furore. The rank and file of the WAAC were drawn mainly from the working and lower-middle classes, and so it was considered particularly important that women from the middle and upper classes of proven ability should be in control. The National Service Department suggested that these class distinctions should be built into the selection procedure. Letters from educated women applying for supervisory posts could not be treated on the same lines as those applying for posts among the rank and file. They suggested drawing up a different form which could be used in the case of educated women.

Official WAAC policy placed considerable emphasis on self-discipline. It was hoped that each individual would respond to the trust placed in her to maintain her personal credit and the reputation of the Corps. But rules were also laid down requiring official permission to go out anywhere; women had to be in by 8 pm; men were not allowed into their recreation rooms; members of the WAAC were not allowed to walk arm in arm with any person; hotels, cafes and restaurants were out of bounds; they could not loiter around the men's camps or barracks when off duty and they were arrested for drunkeness or staying in hotels.

The WAAC's propaganda had to tackle the difficult task of presenting the Army as a respectable and desirable place for a woman. As young, single women were the ideal recruits, many people, especially parents, had to be convinced that although away from home and amongst thousands of men, the women would be properly controlled and looked after and there need be no fears about immorality. Concern about the effects on the femininity of women playing an active role in this male orientated institution, with its strict discipline and uniform, had to be dealt with, as well as the impact on home life. Given the importance of images of home in motivating the fighting man, this point was crucial. And women had to be persuaded that it was their patriotic duty to take the bold step of joining the WAAC. As the written word played an important part in the creation of images during the war, the ways in which press accounts presented the WAAC were important in the drive for recruits. These tried to calm public disquiet by playing down its novel and daring aspects, and attempted to see the role of the women as affirming basic ideas of women's nature and women's place. They also served as prescriptive literature, telling women how they should behave, and challenged opposite trends in women's actual behaviour. Given its ideological importance 'the home' was one of the most predominant themes in WAAC propaganda. Women's position in the army was seen in relation to their capacities as wives, mothers and daughters.

It was always assumed that a woman's first duty was to her family, just as it was a man's to fight for his country. The military authorities did not want women to serve the war effort if it meant abandoning their domestic duties. Women with young children were not encouraged to join; the need of a woman's presence at home was grounds for compassionate discharge. The Duchess of Atholl told a recruiting meeting that if a woman was of suitable age to join the Women's Army she should ask herself: 'Am I doing the best I can for my country's service in my present position?' Many women were not free to go – mothers of young families, women engaged in nursing, munition work, on the land, and in the full-time war work. The appeal was not to them, but to women whose presence was not essential at home or who could be spared from their present employment. She anticipated that many domestic servants would want to join, but they were not to disrupt the households of their employers: 'They should consider their employers' interests so far as this was consonant with their duty to their country and not leave without due notice and consideration.'

One of the central problems with written sources is that so much of the contemporary material had an obvious propaganda purpose – such as boosting morale or encouraging recruits. Descriptions of the women's lives in France present idealised picture, often aimed at reassuring parents and guardians so they would not prevent young women from joining up. Press reports and posters are revealing for their preoccupations and the images of the women they presented – stress was put on the homeliness and comfort of the surroundings, the motherliness of administrators, the servicing role of the women and their good influence on the soldiers morale and morality – but they are not very revealing about either actual conditions or attitudes.

The decision to send women behind the lines in France, was the most novel and morally questionable aspect of the WAAC, but the women were presented as creating a 'home from home' for the men. Mrs Grace Curnock was pleased to tell her readers at Christmas 1917 that: 'British women have a wonderful power – a power which is the keynote of the nation's worldwide greatness, they carry Home wherever they go. At Christmas the men will be made happier from the knowledge that in WAAC camps and YMCA huts, British women are keeping the great festival with all the traditions of home.' The *Glasgow Herald* took a similar line in justifying the work of the WAAC cooks in France: 'The daily routine is carried out with clockwork regularity, and although Army discipline is observed, a homely atmosphere is maintained, an atmosphere obviously appreciated by the soldiers whose food is cooked and served by women.' It was hoped that the presence of the women would inspire the men to fight, by reminding them of the homes for which they were fighting. The women represented comfort and reassurance. To a soldier just down from the line 'to be asked by a nice, clean girl in a nice, clean apron, whether one would have tea or coffee was just like heaven.'

The women might be surrogate mother figures for the soldiers, but they themselves were young, most were in their 20s, and away from home. The army felt conscious of its duty to their parents to look after them, and direct assurances were addressed to parents in the press. By constantly seeing women as the responsibility of their parents, the military officials attempted to calm fears about the women becoming independent, as well as keeping them within the context of the family. The *Manchester Empire* denied certain 'stupid rumours about the conditions under which the women's corps worked in France', and reported that: 'Girls who went out in previous drafts to France have sent back such attractive accounts of their work and life in France that no parents or guardians need have any doubts as to the advisability of allowing girls to go so far from their homes.'

The analogy of the family was used in descriptions of discipline in

France. It was stressed that this was not military style discipline, rather the authorities were '*in loco parentis*'. Much was made of the fact that Administrators were older women, motherly figures. The ideal Administrator was the woman 'with the maternal spirit', whom the girls can easily approach. And in the opinion of *The Common Cause*, an Administrator should be 'mother to the girls under her care, some of whom have never been away from home and are unused to discipline. She should be accessible to the girls at all times, hear complaints, put things right and help them put up with the little difficulties of camp life.' The story of an Administrator who, on return from leave, was greeted by the girls saying: 'It seems as if mother has been away, Ma'am,' was quoted as a good example.

The press acted as a sort of watchdog on the tendency of some Administrators to become carried away by their authority and desire to be 'Army Officers', *John Bull* sharply criticised administrators who strayed from their maternal role and became too disciplinarian. It expressed distaste for some of the WAAC 'officers' who were 'like Germans for discipline.' One lady 'commander' was alleged to address her 'soldier girls' as 'swine' and 'camp-followers'.

The women's surroundings were made to sound as pleasant as possible, well shielded from the horrors and hardship of the battlefield. The description of the first camp in France to be fully staffed by women cooks, in the *Irish Times* becomes quite lyrical: 'The camp itself was quite a village of wooden huts made gay with flower beds and green stripes of lawn. The huts and tents cluster together on the top of a hill, surrounded by undulating downs, fringed with woods, and to the south you can look over sand dunes dotted with busy patches of heath to where the sea lies dazzling blue in the clear atmosphere.' Such reports almost overlooked that the women were part of the war machine, and a few miles away men were fighting it out in the mud and blood of the trenches. Descriptions of the women's living quarters made them sound equally remote from the horror of the war. In contradiction to such propaganda, only oral history can throw light on the women's actual experience.

Wartime propaganda insisted that women recruits were motivated purely by patriotism, but how far had women internalised these values and how far were they acting from reasons of self-actualisation? How did this effect their attitudes to army authority and discipline? War is often alleged to 'foster an atmosphere of national unity',[2] and break down class barriers by creating the opportunity for working class and middle class women to meet on equal terms.[3] To what extent did women become self-conscious about class, were uniform and hard work the great levellers?

Shelia Rowbotham has described how the experience of seeing their friends killed, caused young VADs and WAAC 'privates', to reject middle-class morality.[4] With death so near at hand there was 'no time for the legal niceties of bourgeois marriage.' The personal relationships between the women and the soldiers will be examined in the context of this statement. To what extent did the experience of the war and being able to mix with so many men lead to a loosening of conventional standards of morality amongst WAACs?

Finally through interviews, an assessment has been made of the significance women attached to the experience of being in the WAAC, and its effects on their self-confidence and estimates of their capabilities. Did the opportunity to do a man's job in that most masculine of organisations, the army, make them become restless and dissatisfied with traditional female roles after the war?

The other principal body of sources is the official War Office and WAAC records. These consist mainly of minutes of conferences discussing the decision to form the corps, its organisation and recruitment; circulars from the chief controllers; official reports into conditions and behaviour; army council instructions; corps regulations and war diaries. These are vital for what they reveal about the War Office's attitude to the women's corps, and the hostility of some male officers. They provide detail about chronology, procedures, types of work women undertook, numbers involved, pay, regulations, structures of authority, punishments – the sorts of specific detail where memory is most likely to be hazy. However these all represent the perspective of senior officials. Again the attitudes and experience of the rank and file is the missing dimension oral history can supply.

The purpose of the interviews was not to discover precise dates and details; these could be gleaned with far greater accuracy from documentary sources, but attitudes, moods and situations, which can only be revealed by interviewing. The women remembered a considerable amount about the WAAC and all had vivid personal stories. And although it was important to them, they were not eulogistic or uncritical. In this brief study, it was reassuring that the interviews were reasonably consistent with each other and with other sources.

Perhaps the most interesting question is why did women want to join the army in the first place? The WAAC represented for many women a longed-for opportunity to become more directly involved in the war. All the women interviewed were already working, and financial incentives were not mentioned. They all described themselves as patriotic, and given the emphasis on patriotism at this time and feelings of social guilt which can so easily be aroused in wartime, it must have been very difficult to resist these pressures. Within the context of taking the war very seriously, women felt unfulfilled and dissatisfied with their powerlessness to do anything they considered really important for the war effort. Brothers and boyfriends, assured by posters that 'your country needs you', left to join the army and with fighting elevated to the highest chivalric virtue in representations of the war, women felt excluded. In this sense the WAAC appeared to be an answer to their needs and because of the high status of the army, women saw the WAAC as much more significant than any other form of war work. It appeared to be a chance to really have an impact on events, to become part of something important:

> 'It was a wonderful feeling that you were doing something, that you really belonged. Now this is it, and the war would end any moment sort of thing.'

> 'Like Kitchener said, everyone was wanted sort of idea . . . I mean it was breaking away from everyday life.'

> 'I thought it was a much bigger war effort joining that . . . I felt the army was a much bigger war job than what I was doing in the naval dockyards you see.'

A woman who worked as a clerk with the London Bus Company, described how she and her friends greeted the formation of the WAAC with enthusiasm:

> 'We wanted to do something, really, do something for the war, because after all we were just in a clerical job, we weren't doing anything as we thought vital for the war.'

Releasing a man added to the feeling that joining the WAAC would be doing something important, one woman 'wanted to do the same jobs as the boys' and others shared this feeling although it was tinged by the personal sorrow of the war. Becoming involved was a way of coping:

> 'We thought we'd be on the spot. And the advertisements said release a man for the firing line, which we thought was very heroic, and of course things were going very badly for us . . . everyday there were casualty lists in the papers and we'd look down them for someone we knew.'

There was also a general feeling that men should be doing work women could do in time of war:

> 'I thought it would be helping if the women came forward. It would relieve the men, the women could do the cooking and that sort of thing which would release the men for other jobs which were necessary.'

These excerpts indicate the power of the patriotic cause. In this, the women were living up to what was expected of them, but the WAAC had another powerful attraction. It represented a unique opportunity for adventure, to do something extraordinary, which was only made possible because of the war and the chance it provided to leave home. Having talked about her patriotism, one woman went on to say that she'd 'only joined to go to France.' Another, who was on Home Service said she was terribly disappointed that she did not go abroad. If she had known she was going to be on home service she would not have joined up. Asked why she was so keen to go abroad, she replied: 'For the experience, I wanted it for the experience.' One of the women in her draft pretended to be hysterical after she found out they were not going to France, in order to get discharged.

Lady Balfour pointed out that: 'There was something very wonderful in going to a post near the Front', and as her boat neared Boulogne one woman recalled that she 'was blissfully happy at the thought that I should at last be "in the war".' A space was created by the war's disruption of normal life for women to have some independence. They could live away from home, and although women had to accept official discipline and work hard, at least they had escaped family constraints. And despite hardships and problems, this independence was exhilarating: 'For two years we worked long hours seven days a week, we were cold, dirty and badly fed. Did we care? Not a bit! We were young, we kept on falling in and out of love, and we have got our fingers into the war pie.'

The war presented an opportunity for women to escape other private tyrannies. In 1918 the numbers of domestic servants had considerably decreased. These women seized the chance to leave the loneliness and strict, personalised controls of their employers' households and enjoy the relative freedom of war work. They came forward to fill the domestic section, the largest of the WAAC, because as uniformed women 'soldiers', living in hostels and working for their country rather than individuals, many of them were happier than they had been in any former situation.

It was the military aspect of the Corps, the chance to 'be soldiers', was one of the most attractive aspects for a group of WAACs questioned by the Vicar of Ripon about their views on recruiting, because: 'They know their own class and what will appeal to the same sort of people as themselves.' They suggested route marches through the districts where recruits were being sought. The women marching should be dressed in their uniform as smartly as possible, and drill on the march should be smart and good, there should be singing and a lady should make a good, short, stirring speech at the end. The vicar noticed that there was no suggested appeal to patriotism or patriotic motives, but supposed that this was taken for granted. This suggests that these women were most keen on the so-called 'unfeminine' aspects of the Corps, which had been played down in the press.

All the women frequently faced fierce opposition from their families, and had great difficulty getting them to accept their decision to join the WAAC. One woman had an 'awful to do' with her parents, and 'they wouldn't sign the papers for a long while'. Her brother also objected because 'it wasn't right that a girl should leave home,' and he also felt it wasn't respectable: 'Girls that go abroad, they aren't thought anything of.' A woman's first duty was to her home, just as it was a man's to fight for his country:

'My mother didn't like it at all, neither did my father, and my brother, he was an officer, he joined up very early in the War, and they thought it was the right and proper thing that he should go out and if necessary die for his country. But not me. It simply was a general idea that it wasn't nice women who did that sort of thing.'

She also spoke about the double standard inherent in their attitude:

'They didn't mind me nearly killing myself doing that [working seven days a week in an office and doing work for the Women's Volunteer Reserve] but when it came to the army they did not like it!'

Furthermore, the purpose of the WAAC, to release men, had the effect of provoking widespread hostility. People in England accused them of 'making widows and orphans . . . when we went out to France the people we replaced were sent up the line!' This may have been one reason behind the spread of rumours of WAAC immorality. Nor were they popular with the soldiers:

'You can imagine the men didn't welcome us because they were being sent into the line when we came. When we first went they didn't want us, definitely.'

One woman remembered a specific instance of resentment:

'I know of a case where a behind the lines soldier definitely tried to get a girl, kind of made it evident that she had done something in her work. It was quite possible in the work we were doing you see, to implicate someone else.'

Eventually, the men did come round to accepting the women. This was mainly because those whom they were replacing left for the front as soon as the women had learnt the work, and those left behind in the offices were either invalided or physically unfit for active service so were not threatened by the women. In fact they welcomed their company and the concerts and dances which relieved the monotony of army life.

The powerful hold of the concept of duty severely restricted any expression of opposition during the war. Consequently the men's hostility did not cause the women to question their own role. Often they felt sad that the men had to go, but never critical: 'I don't think we took all that much notice (of resentment) because we felt we were doing what we were asked to do.' Another woman was more emphatic:

> 'In those days we thought it was dreadful for a man not to want to go, we thought of him as a coward. We had no sympathy for them because we were releasing them, we thought it was our duty.'

Both women said they felt differently about this after the war, when they realised how terrible the conditions in the trenches were, but at the time they had a more idealised concept of war.

Women came across a different kind of resentment from men whom they were not replacing. This stemmed more from dislike of the women's presence in the all-male atmosphere of the army. A woman who was a waitress in the Sergeants' Mess spoke about their attitudes:

> 'They wouldn't put themselves out to do anything . . . well you see that was their resentfulness because women were not supposed to do all these things . . . they didn't like the idea of women soldiers sort of thing.'

All the women remembered working very long, hard hours. A 12 hour day with a half day off per week was usual for clerks; drivers and domestics often worked longer. However, they were all prepared to work long hours because of the war, and there were few complaints about the work. Their capacity to work hard and their efficiency were seen as instrumental in gaining acceptance from the men. Furthermore, having some idea of the experiences of the men at the front made the women accept poor conditions. It became so cold driving that one woman lost some of her toes from frostbite, but she was very stoical and 'thought about the boys, our own hardships were nothing, compared to theirs. They had no home comforts.' However, there were complaints about the food, which all agreed was terrible. Any spare money was spent in cafes, otherwise they would be permanently hungry. Uniform was another area of dispute. Unpopular brown collars were changed for white ones before the women went to the towns, and they had ways of getting round the regulation that dresses had to be nine inches from the ground, even to the extent of making them a 'respectable length' and then cutting them off, because they kept trailing in the mud and wet.

There was a sense that some of the regulations which governed their lives were unnecessary and these were evaded. Staying out late without a pass and trying to get back into the camp without being seen were common events. Army etiquette demanded that the 'rank and file' should not mix with officers and this was the most resentful rule of all. Officers had more money and social status, and the rule was frequently flouted. If they were seen together the men and women would get into trouble. To avoid this meant going out after dark and having a private room in a hotel if they wanted a meal together, a practice which could have contributed towards the rumours about immorality. Flouting some of the rules was consistent with high spirits and feeling of independence because of being away from home but it did not constitute a direct challenge to authority. None of the informants had any experience of serious cases of disobedience. Administrators were spoken about as either rather distant figures or as more motherly and accessible – 'like matrons in a girls school'.[5] Those who tried to model themselves too closely on male officers tended to be more unpopular but their authority was accepted. Punishments – women could be fined or confined to barracks – were endured without complaint, even if women felt they had been treated pettily or unfairly.

The women were well insulated from the harsh realities of the war. They had little contact with men from the front line, but occasionally when they did witness the brutal side of army life, there was the same fatalistic acceptance of authority:

'I drove for the Assistant Provost Marshall for a while . . . in this one case there was a boy, such a nice boy and he had run away, and they had to arrest him. In those days if you were cowardly you were shot. We picked him up, I knew what it was and I was crying my eyes out. He said: "It's alright miss, it was my fault, I shouldn't have run away but I couldn't help it." He was going to be shot.'

Promotion from the ranks to the position of administrator was most uncommon. None of the women knew of any cases. Some of them, however, were made forewomen, the equivalent of a noncommissioned officer. A woman who regularly voiced the general complaints about food, was told she was not promoted because she was identified as a ringleader. Another did not want promotion because it would have meant giving up driving, and that was what she had come to do. Rank did not have the same allure for women as it did for men. The lack of promotion to administrator level is consistent with the war office's view that these should be older, middle and upper-class women, with experience of working with women. This, they felt, would ensure proper discipline and that sufficient attention be given to the women's welfare.

It is evident that there was a high degree of class consciousness in the WAAC. Although references were made to 'extraordinary friendships' which could not have been formed in England and to women 'mixing well', attitudes reflected the rigid class structures of Edwardian England. Forewomen tended to stick together, and kept their distance from the women they were in charge of, and clerks tended not to have much to do with the household staff. The latter were generally women who had been in service or worked in shops, part of their job being to service the other women. Women doing the same jobs would be accommodated together:

> 'When I was in Folkestone we had an awful lot of women from Glasgow with a frightful accent, you couldn't understand a word they said. And they were all going as bakeresses and I think they probably did put them in a camp like to like . . .They did segregate us.'

If anything unpleasant happened suspicion fell on the Household Staff:

> 'If something was stolen they would immediately say it was the domestic staff.'

> 'One girl had unfortunately to be sent up to the isolation hospital. She was dirty. It was horrible . . . she had got insects on her, she had never changed her clothes. But she wasn't clerical of course, she was probably a household.'

These divisions were reflected in attitudes about work. A group of women sent to camp to be trained as clerks provoked resentment because they were not considered good enough:

'They were all under us its true, but they really didn't know their job you see. We had to teach them and some of them, they weren't fit to be clerks. We couldn't send them in and say these girls are no good to us, you see . . . Well they couldn't add up and things like that you see, the kind of clerical work that was needed. Our lot were girls who had just come from College, they had not even been out to business at all, and they were rather a high standard . . . They were really rather a nice crowd of girls. Then we got this other lot that were sent for other duties icluding clerical, and they were not the same type.'

'What type were they?'

'Well, do you know Brixton? That type of person . . . Well I think a lot of them had been in service quite frankly.'

The oral evidence illustrates how class position determined expectations as well as the degree of interest and excitement a woman experienced in the WAAC. A woman who was a 'living in' mother's help before the war was only qualified to be a domestic. Her memories were of the different messes where she waitressed and kitchens where she scrubbed the pots and pans. But she liked her work, and enjoyed making things nice and shiny and she felt she was helping. Whereas a woman who knew how to drive and could afford the fee to take the RAC Certificate in mechanics which was required because the women had to do their own maintenance, had no such mundane experiences. No day was alike for her, she wanted to go up near the front line, and she drove officers and generals all over the lines of communication.

Despite the fears of civilians and press statements meant to counteract them, the women had the opportunity to mix relatively freely with men, for the army could not hope to supervise them all the time. However women had it impressed upon them that their behaviour reflected on the honour of the corps, and rules were laid down about how late they could stay out and where they could go in their free time. Due to the number of men around and the fact that many were in transit, women tended to go out with many different men although some did become engaged. Social life revolved around walks, visits to cafes and occasional dances and concerts organised by the YMCA. None of the informants talked about having sexual relationships, although this was an area that women were still reticent about. Many had been surprised and upset when they discovered the rumours about their immoral behaviour, or if some of the soldiers made assumptions about them:

> 'Some of the men we met in France were getting a bit fresh you see and of course we were very prudish . . . and we ticked them off. And they said "what are you? we thought you were WAACs . . . are you Church Army?" "No", we said, "we are WAACs." "Do you have a sister?" we said to one of them. "Yes, but not a WAAC thank God." . . . There must have been some gossip about us.'

Assumptions about immorality reflected the notion that women who left home, particularly to become part of a male dominated world like the army, must be sexually suspect. It was not accepted that their motives were patriotic, they went to be with men. 'People, thought we were awful people, camp followers.' 'Of course they thought we were all coming home with illegitimate children, once we got out there with men.' 'A lot of people really thought we were a really bad lot, they had no doubt about it. French people had not the slightest doubt what we were there for.' When they came home on leave women would draw their dresses away from them on public transport, and a woman was refused her old job back at the end of the war because the boss 'wouldn't employ a woman who had followed the men to France.' Even those women, who saw themselves as respectable and patriotic, to others were beyond the pale because they had temporarily stepped out of accepted female roles.

There also appears to have been an element of sexual jealousy, along with the other reason already mentioned for the rumours. When the WAACs arrived at camp in Richborough the local girls hated them. Prior to the WAACs arrival there used to be dances in the village with the soldiers and they were all having a good time. The WAACs were butting in, and were seen as competition. Village girls were not allowed into the camp dances, but the WAACs could go to the dances in the village. Those out in France made women back home uneasy because many of them 'had got their men out in France. Well, they thought they were meeting the WAACs and having a good time with them, and that sort of thing . . .' Given these stereotypes, they would be predisposed to believe adverse stories about the WAACs. Undoubtedly, sexual relations was one of the most sensitive areas for WAACs public image. Misunderstandings were another possible explanation. One woman recalled how the change involved in going to France affected her periods. She did not have one for three months, and although she knew she hadn't 'done anything' others might suspect her of being pregnant.

All the informants did know of one or two cases of pregnancy. There was a feeling that the women involved must have 'already been that type' or else they were ignorant. For most it was the first time away from home, but women were not given any information about sex by the WAAC. Nevertheless if they did become pregnant they were blamed for it:

> 'Now I had been working with this girl. I was quite innocent of misbehaviour really, I didn't realise that she was going to have a baby . . . she was packed off without a character, just turned out . . . she had no clothes for the baby, so there was a whip round from the officers, people gave her some money for material and we made up some clothes for the baby, and she went into the workhouse . . . I felt very sorry for her. She wasn't a bad girl. She was stupid. She knew who the father was but he couldn't be traced. . . . He was out of her class altogether. . . . He had been a college boy and she was just a nobody.'

This illustrates the risks for women of 'sexual freedom'. It also indicates that although the official policy on pregnancy was quite liberal – that is women were to be discharged from the WAAC but their welfare was not to be lost sight of and those in need were to be given some financial help – it did not always work that way in practice.

Despite the fact that they had a lot of contact with men and the opportunity to do so if they wished, it appears that double standards of morality, risk of pregnancy, ignorance and their own attitudes and desire for 'respectability' all conspired to make women in the WAAC maintain conventional morality.

It was clear from the interviews that the experience of joining the WAAC was an exceptional event in the women's lives. In wartime the role of the fighting man became important, and the women, accepting this male defined value system, felt it was a privilege to be allowed into the exclusively male world of the army and work to support the men at the Front. However they accepted that this was a temporary occurrence, because of the demands of the war effort. After demobilisation the women went back to the same kind of work they were doing before joining up. Although the WAAC had official schemes to help women find employment, none of those interviewed remembered benefiting from them.

The women felt that the experience of being in the army had given them greater self-confidence. They saw what women could do and that 'they were equal to any emergency', but it did not effect fundamental changes in their opinions. Those who had supported the women's suffrage movement and questioned women's subordination before the war continued to do so both in the WAAC and after 1918. One woman had organised a protest to the army authorities about discrimination over pay. Men conscripted from the Central Telegraph Office got their full civilian and army pay, whereas women only received the latter. But those who were not interested in women's subordination did not change their opinions on account of their war work.

It was very striking that, paradoxically for all the sorrow, suffering, hard work, and physical discomfort and even danger, of the war the women remembered the WAAC as a 'wonderful experience'. It is ironic that it needed a catastrophe like the Great War to break the bonds which tied these women to the home and give them the chance to enjoy doing something different and unusual. Above all it was a rare opportunity to live and work with other women and it was this companionship that she was remembered most fondly and valued most highly by all the informants, rather than the chance to do a man's job or the opportunity to have relationships with men with relatively few restrictions.

'I think it was the finest thing, and we all say that, my crowd, it was the most marvellous thing that ever happened because there was a wonderful comradeship that you never lose, it a marvellous feeling, and you meet each other and its still there. It's a lovely feeling that you went through so much together, I think it was wonderful.'

In assessing the position of the women who joined the WAAC, a number of influencing factors has to be taken into account. Positions of authority were largely determined by class, and central to this was the maternal relationship between the middle and upper-class Administrators and the working-class women of the rank and file. Then tension between women attempting to conform to a male-defined value system, and the military authorities' rejection to their bid for full participation in the Army, moulded the structure of the corps as women pressed the War Office for a better deal. In addition they had to face hostility from men in their work and deal with a derogatory public reputation. But despite the low status and lack of respect for the WAAC, it was also a real, if temporary, chance for women to escape their family constraints, enjoy living and working with other women, and to demonstrate their stamina and bravery by enduring long working hours and tough conditions with added dangers such as frequent air raids.

The WAAC was disbanded in May 1920. Altogether some 41 000 women had served the corps. With the war over, life for them returned to normal. Women were now accused of taking jobs which men, particularly disabled soldiers, could do: 'The Army in peace has no place for women.'[6] The position of the WAAC reveals the army to be a microcosm of wider power relationships based on class and gender. Women in the WAACs did enter a previously exclusively male institution, but rather than this representing any step forward in the struggle for women's rights, it tended to reproduce, and not to challenge, the sexual balance of power in British society.

Notes

1. Arthur Mawick, *The Deluge*, 1965.
2. *Report of the Commission of Enquiry, Appointed by the Minister of Labour to Enquire into Cases of Alleged Immoral Conduct*. 20 March 1918. Women's Collection Army 3.28.2, Imperial War Museum.
3. Marion Kozak, review of 'Women at War' exhibition at the Imperial War Museum. *History Workshop Journal*, no. 4, Autumn 1977, p. 239.
4. S. Rowbotham *Hidden From History*, 1974, p. 1.
5. The WAAC was not allowed to adopt the ranks of the male army and had to use its own terms. At its head were the Chief Controller and Chief Controller (overseas). They had a staff of Deputy Controllers and Administrators who looked after the women in their camps and hostels. The equivalent of an NCO was a Forewoman and the rank-and-file were called workers.
6. See Report of the Women War Workers Resettlement Committee 18 November 1918, Women's Collective Army 3 31.2 Imperial War Museum. 'Overseas Settlement of Members', Wo 162/54 Public Records Office.

Further Reading

1. General Books for the Economic and Social Background to the Period

Noreen Branson and Margot Heinemann, *Britain in the Nineteen Thirties* (London: Panther Books, 1973).

Eric Hopkins, *A Social History of the English Working Classes* (London: Edward Arnold, 1979).

Arthur Marwick, *The Deluge: British Society and the First World War* (Harmondsworth: Penguin, 1965).

Charles Mowat, *Britain Between the Wars: 1918–1940* (London: Methuen, 1968).

Pat Thane, *The Foundations of the Welfare State* (London: Longman, 1982).

Paul Thompson, *The Edwardians: The Remaking of British Society* (London: Weidenfeld & Nicolson, 1984). (Uses oral material.)

2. Women's World in the Period

Most of the early books have recently been reprinted. A few are by modern scholars.

Ruth Adam, *A Woman's Place: 1910–1975* (London: Chatto & Windus, 1975).

Lady Bell, *At the Works: A Study of a Manufacturing Town* (1907) (London: Virago, 1980).

Clementina Black, *Married Women's Work* (1915) (London: Virago, 1983).

Gail Braybon, *Women Workers in the First World War* (London: Barnes & Noble, 1981).

Leonore Davidoff, *The Best Circles, Society, Etiquette and the Season* (London: Croom Helm, 1973).

Leonore Davidoff, 'The Separation of Home and Work? Landladies and Lodgers in Victorian and Edwardian England', in S. Burman (ed.) *Fit Work for Women* (London: Croom Helm, 1979).

Margaret Llewellyn Davies (ed.), *Life As We Have Known It* (1931) (London: Virago, 1977).

Margaret Llewellyn Davies (ed.), *Maternity: Letters from Working Women* (1915) (London: Virago, 1978).

Carol Dyhouse, *Girls Growing Up in Later Victorian and Edwardian England* (London: Croom Helm, 1980).

Barbara Drake, *Women in Trade Unions* (1921) (London: Virago, 1984).

John Gillis, *For Better, For Worse: British Marriages 1600 to the Present* (Oxford: Oxford University Press, 1985). (Part Three).

Diana Gittins, *Fair Sex: Family Size and Structure 1900–1939* (London: Hutchinson, 1982).

Miriam Glucksman 'In a Class of their own? Women Workers in the New Industries in Inter-war Britain', *Feminist Review* (forthcoming).

Cicely Hamilton, *Marriage as A Trade* (1909) (London: Women's Press, 1981).

Lee Holcombe, *Victorian Ladies at Work: Middle Class Working Women 1850–1914* (Newton Abbot: David & Charles, 1973).

Angela John, *By the Sweat of their Brow: Women Workers at Victorian Coal Mines* (London: Routledge & Kegan Paul, 1984).

Angela V. John (ed.), *Unequal Opportunities: Women's Employment in England 1800–1918* (Oxford: Blackwell, 1986).

Jane Lewis (ed.), *Women's Experience of Home and Family, 1850–1940* (Oxford: Blackwell, 1986).

Jane Lewis, *Women in England: 1870–1950* (University of Indiana, 1984).

Ellen Mappen, *Helping Women at Work, The Women's Industrial Council 1889–1914* (London: Hutchinson, 1985).

Maud Pember Reeves, *Round About a Pound A Week* (1913) (London: Virago, 1979).

Elizabeth Roberts, *A Woman's Place: An Oral History of Working-Class Women: 1890–1940* (Oxford: Oxford University Press, 1984).

Jacqueline Sarsby, 'Sexual Segregation in the Pottery Industry', *Feminist Review* 21, 1985.

Margery Spring Rice, *Working-Class Wives* (1939) (London: Virago, 1981).

Paul Thompson 'Women in the Fishing: the roots of power between the sexes', *Comparative Studies in Society and History*, vol. 27, no. 1, 1985.

Martha Vicinus, *Independent Women: Work and Community for Single Women 1850–1920* (Chicago: University of Chicago Press and London: Virago, 1985).

3. Modern Approaches to Women's Lives and Work

Cynthia Cockburn 'The Material of Male Power', *Feminist Review*, 9, 1981. (Women and Printing).

Diana Gittins, *The Family in Question: Changing Households and Familiar Ideologies* (London: Macmillan, 1985).

Eva Gamarnikow, David Morgan, June Purvis and Daphne Taylorson (eds) *Gender, Class and Work* (London: Heinemann, 1983).
George Joseph, *Women at Work: The British Experience* (London: Philip Allan) 1983.
Ann Oakley, *Subject Women* (London: Fontana, 1982).
A. Philips and Barbara Taylor 'Sex and Skill: Notes towards a Feminist Economics', *Feminist Review* 6, 1980.
Louise Tilly and Joan Scott, *Women, Work and Family* (New York: Winston, Rinehart & Holt, 1978).
Jeffrey Weeks, *Sex, Politics and Society: The Regulation of Sexuality since. 1800* (London: Longman, 1981).
Cynthia White, *Women's Magazines: 1693–1968* (London: Michael Joseph, 1970).
Jackie West (ed.) *Work, Women and the Labour Market* (London: Routledge & Kegan Paul, 1982).

4. Oral History

Mary Chamberlain, *Fen Women: A Portrait of Women in an English Village* (London: Routledge & Kegan Paul, 1983).
Stephen Humphries, *The Handbook of Oral History: Recording Life Stories*, The Inter-Action Creative Community Projects Series, ed. Ed Berman (1984).
Paul Thompson, *The Voice of the Past: Oral History* (Oxford: Oxford University Press, 1978).
Oral History. This is the official journal of the Oral History Society which has been published since 1971 from the Department of Sociology, University of Essex. Of particular interest is volume 5, no. 2 (Autumn 1977) which is specifically concerned with Women's History.

5. Autobiography

There is a growing number of published accounts of women's lives in this period. The following is only a selection.

Vera Brittain, *Testament of Youth: An Autobiographical Study of the Years 1900–1925* (London: Virago, 1978).
John Burnett, *Useful Toil: Autobiographies of Working People From the 1820s to the 1920s* (Harmondsworth: Allen Lane, 1974).
Doris N. Chew, *Ada Nield Chew: the Life and Writings of a Working Woman* (London: Virago, 1982).
Kathleen Dayus, *Where There's Life* (London: Virago, 1985).
Winifred Foley, *A Child in the Forest* (London, Fontana, 1981).
Helen Forrester, *Two Pence to Cross the Mersey* (London: Fontana, 1981).
Helen Forrester, *Liverpool Miss* (London: Fontana/Collins, 1982).

Hannah Mitchell, *The Hard Way Up* (London: Virago, 1977).

Margaret Powell, *Below Stairs* (London: Pan Books, 1968).

Joe Robinson, *The Life and Times of Francie Nichol of South Shields* (London: Fontana, 1975).

Jean Rennie, *Every Other Sunday: the Diary of a Kitchen Maid* (London: St. Martin's Press, 1981).

Angela Rodancy, *A London Childhood* (London: Virago, 1985).

Index